BY THE EDITORS OF CONSUMER GUIDE®

The CAMERA handbook

BEEKMAN HOUSE
New York

CONTENTS

10 9 8 7 6 5 4 3 2 1

Library of Congress
  Catalog Card Number: 82-61172
ISBN: 0-517-382008

This edition published by:
Beekman House
Distributed by Crown Publishers, Inc.
One Park Avenue
New York, New York 10016

Writer: Kim Brady
Artist: Clarence A. Moberg
Technical Consultant: John R. Grimes
Front Cover Photograph: Robert E. Mayer
Back Cover Photograph: Robert McQuilkin

3   Introduction

PART 1: EXPOSURE

4-5   THE CAMERA METER—Light is the key to perfect pictures

6-7   FILM SPEED—Choose your film to fit the light

8-9   PROGRAM MODE—Capture the candid moments

10-11   APERTURE-PREFERRED MODE—The emphasis is up to you

12-13   SHUTTER-PREFERRED MODE—Catch the action, show the motion

14-15   MANUAL MODE—Take control for perfect pictures

16-17   EXPOSURE COMPENSATION—Use uneven light to your advantage

18-19   THE EXPOSURE MEMORY LOCK—Move close to read the light

20-21   SILHOUETTES—Use light and form for dramatic effect

22-23   MULTIPLE EXPOSURES—Repetition creates the impact

PART 2: SEEING THE PICTURE

24-25   FRAMING AND COMPOSITION—Pay attention to what you see

26-27   LIGHT, DARK, AND COLOR—Use contrast to create meaning

28-29   THE NORMAL LENS—Take the picture as you see it

30-31   TELEPHOTO LENSES—Emphasize the essentials

32-33   WIDE-ANGLE LENSES—Take a wider look at the world

34-35   CLOSE-UPS—Concentrate on the details

36-37   SMALL APERTURES—Keep the whole picture sharp

38-39   LARGE APERTURES—Put the accent where you want it

40-41   SPECIAL FOCUS TECHNIQUES—Record important details sharply

PART 3: ACTION AND TIME

42-43   FAST SHUTTER SPEEDS—Freeze the action

44-45   SLOW SHUTTER SPEEDS—Show the flow of the motion

46-47   PANNING—Move with the action

48-49   TIME EXPOSURES—Prolong the impression

50-51   THE SELF-TIMER—Get into the picture

PART 4: FILTERS AND FLASH

52-53   POLARIZING AND CORRECTION FILTERS—Discover their effects

54-55   SPECIAL-EFFECTS FILTERS—Experiment for many moods

56-57   ON-CAMERA FLASH—Add light to the picture

58-59   OFF-CAMERA FLASH—Extend the light, soften the shadows

PART 5: TECHNIQUES

60-61   CAMERA HANDLING—Basic photography techniques

62-64   Glossary

INTRODUCTION

Photography is the art of seeing—and the art of capturing what you see on film. To take good photographs, you need both imagination and know-how, the seeing eye and the technician's hand. This book shows you how all the parts of the camera—exposure meter, viewfinder, controls, lenses—work together, and how you can use them to take the best pictures you've ever seen.

The photographs in this book give you a wide variety of examples. They show you what kind of pictures you can take in different camera modes, what different films can do, how your camera's exposure meter reads the light. You'll see how you can get the best exposure in difficult lighting situations, and how you can use special kinds of exposures to get dramatic effects.

Look at your camera's standard lens; this is the normal lens, and you can use it to record scenes exactly as you see them. Then look at the other lenses you can use with your camera—telephotos, wide-angles, close-ups, and zooms. All of them change the camera's perception; all of them will give you different pictures. This book tells you how and when to use each lens to get great pictures, whatever you're photographing—people, places, sports, wildlife, or any interesting part of the world around you.

Exposure—the way the light strikes the film—is the key to good photographs, and this book shows you how you can use the principles of exposure to get exactly the pictures you want. By adjusting the size of the opening in the lens—the aperture—you can control the focus in your pictures, to keep everything in the scene sharp or to emphasize one subject. By adjusting the shutter speed, you can control the way your camera records motion—to freeze fast action, to blur a moving subject, to get exciting and impressive photographs of sports, children playing, fireworks, families, and every part of your fast-moving, changing, growing world.

The pictures in this book show you how to use all of these camera parts and controls to create just the picture you want,

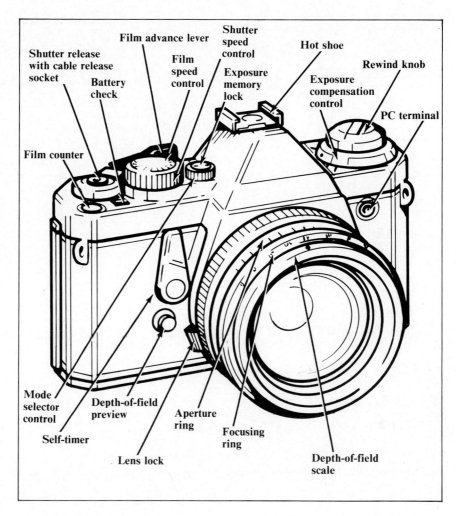

every time. And because the basics aren't always enough, you'll also find discussions of camera accessories that can make the difference between a mediocre picture and a great one—filters, electronic flash units, and special effects that can turn an ordinary photograph into a memorable one.

You'll find a variety of useful information—tips, technical instructions, ideas, and critical comments—in a form that's easy to understand and easy and interesting to use. Some of the techniques explained here apply to several controls or parts of the camera, because all of the camera's parts are interrelated. Other tips are more useful for one particular situation, and are discussed in the most appropriate section.

This book is a handbook—read the whole book and you'll understand how photography works. But you don't have to read the whole book to understand the discussion about any one part or use of the camera—skip around; you'll find that you can put these tips to work with your very next shot. The only background knowledge you need is how to operate your 35mm camera, as explained in your camera instruction manual.

Together, the pictures and text in this book show you how easy it is to use your camera for the pictures you want—pictures that are both technically excellent and exciting to look at. The more you use this book, the more you'll learn—and the better your pictures will be.

THE CAMERA METER
Light is the key to perfect pictures

The photographer looked at this house and saw shapes, colors, details; her eyes adjusted to the light and shade in the scene to let her see it clearly. When you take a picture, the camera must make the same kind of adjustments to the light that your eyes make. To do this, it uses a built-in light meter, or exposure meter. The meter measures the light in the scene and tells you what camera settings will give you a properly exposed picture.

The exposure of a photograph depends on the amount of light that reaches the film through the camera lens—how much light, controlled by the lens aperture or f-stop, and for how long, controlled by the shutter speed. The sensitivity or speed of the film also affects exposure. The camera meter works with three important controls—the f-stop ring, the shutter speed control, and the ISO/ASA dial—to identify the camera settings that will give you the best exposure.

To use the camera meter, you must tell it how sensitive the film is; you do this by setting the ISO/ASA control for the proper speed. Once you give it this information, the meter measures the light that's reflected off the objects in your picture, and then identifies an exposure that will give you the best average reading for the whole scene.

The meter is easy to use; just turn it on and look through the viewfinder. In the manual mode, the meter tells you whether you need more or less light to get a good exposure; you adjust the f-stop and shutter speed to provide the right amount of light. Automatic cameras adjust these settings for you.

You can use any combination of settings as long as the amount of light stays the same—either open the aperture one stop and decrease the time by using the next faster shutter speed, or close the aperture one stop and increase the time by using the next slower shutter speed. By varying the settings this way, you can stop action, blur movement, or select the depth of field you want in your pictures. All of these choices are discussed in this book.

- Pointing your camera directly at the sun or another strong light source can dazzle the meter. If this happens, wait a few minutes to let the meter recover before taking a picture.

- When the sun is shining at an angle to the scene, it creates a strong cross light, with very bright whites and very deep shadows. To keep detail in the shadows, point the camera away from large areas of white to take a meter reading. When there's extreme contrast between light and dark, take more than one picture—the first shot at the indicated settings, and two more at half an f-stop more and half an f-stop less exposure.

- If your subject is strongly backlighted, an overall exposure reading will result in a too-light background and a too-dark subject. To prevent this, take your light reading directly from your subject, without including the source of the light. If you can't get close enough to take a direct reading, take a reading from an object near you that has similar light and shadow, or simply point the camera straight down at the ground.

- When you're photographing people, the skin tones are the most important, so take your exposure reading from your subjects' faces. If you can't get close enough or you don't want to distract them, hold your hand in the same kind of light and take a reading from it.

- Shooting on a cloudy, overcast day can create problems of high contrast, because the sky is the brightest thing in your picture. To prevent underexposure, point the camera down away from the sky, and don't include large areas of sky in the frame when taking an exposure reading.

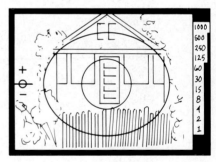

Read your instruction manual to find out what kind of meter your camera has and what exposure information it displays. Averaging meters read the light in the entire scene and average it. Center-weighted meters read the light in the whole scene, but put greater emphasis on an area covering about 40 percent of the frame, in the center (oval line). Spot meters read only a small circle at the center of the frame (inner circle). Some camera meters can be used in more than one mode.

FILM SPEED
Choose your film to fit the light

Taking a well-exposed picture isn't always easy. You'll encounter a wide variety of lighting situations, and your subjects won't always be holding still. The many types of film on the market can help you meet these challenges.

These pictures were taken in very different circumstances, with very different films—the dancers with a fast film, the classic car with a slow one. Films are described in terms of speed as a measure of their sensitivity to light—the higher the ISO/ASA rating a film has, the less light is needed to record an image on it. A film with an ISO/ASA rating of 25 is less sensitive—slower—than one with an ISO/ASA of 200.

Film speed is an important factor in determining correct exposure. The ISO/ASA control tells the camera meter how sensitive the film is; when you set the ISO/ASA number on the dial, the meter can judge how much light will form an image and what combinations of shutter speed and f-stop will give you a good exposure.

Slow color films have an ISO/ASA of 25 to 32; normal films are rated 64 to 160. Films with a rating of ISO/ASA 200 and higher are called fast films. All of these films have certain advantages, and you can improve your pictures by using the film that works best for each situation.

Slow films are best for subjects that aren't moving, or where the light is bright; they can also be used when you want to show motion. They have rich color and detail, and give you the sharpest image quality. Fast films are used in situations where you couldn't take a picture with slow film—where your subject is moving, or the light is low, or you want to use the smallest lens opening and the fastest shutter speed possible. Picture quality is not as good with fast films—colors are less brilliant, and your pictures tend to look grainy. In very low light, the background may disappear entirely.

The film speed control is usually located on the top right of the camera, around the shutter speed control or the film advance lever (top), or on the top left side, around the rewind knob (bottom). By setting the film's ISO/ASA on this dial, you tell your camera how to judge the amount of light necessary to record an image.

● ISO/ASA 25 film is good for close-ups, but the best film for all-around use is ISO/ASA 64. Carry ISO/ASA 400 film for pictures at night or dusk, in dim light, and for stage performances; fast film is also useful for taking pictures with a telephoto lens, even in bright sunlight. For the best pictures, always use the slowest film the situation permits.

● Closely allied to film speed is film type. Some slide films are made specifically for shooting in daylight and some are made for artificial lighting. Always use the right type of film for the light— daylight film for natural light from the sun or with electronic flash, tungsten film for incandescent lighting, stage lighting, or display lighting. The fastest tungsten film is ISO/ASA 160. There is no film made for use in fluorescent light; to take pictures in this kind of light, you need a color correction filter. Filters are discussed later in this book; the Glossary

entry for "Fluorescent light" provides more detail.

● High-speed transparency films can be given increased ISO/ASA ratings by "push processing." This means that you can shoot a roll of film with your camera's ISO/ASA control set higher than the film's actual rating, and have the film specially processed to make up for the difference. Push processing won't give you high-quality pictures, but it can be useful where you need extra film speed.

● High contrast is often a problem in low-light situations. To get an accurate exposure reading, take your reading from an area of the scene that does not include a light source; you can use the camera's exposure memory lock for this, as discussed later in this book.

When your subject is spotlighted, get up close and take your meter reading from the spotlighted area, not including the dark background; or take a reading from a similarly lit object closer to you. If you can't get close enough, take an overall reading and allow one-half to one f-stop less exposure. Try several exposures to make sure you get a good picture.

PROGRAM MODE
Capture the candid moments

The best pictures are often not the result of careful staging; they're spontaneous—one-chance shots that may never happen again. In this picture, the photographer caught one moment, one pattern, in a constantly changing situation. He had no time to analyze the exposure needed; the gestures and movements of the people were changing the picture too fast. The important thing here was capturing the actions and the expressions at the right instant.

The program mode is ideal for this kind of photography. When your camera is set in the program mode—sometimes called automatic or auto—it automatically chooses the correct shutter speed and f-stop needed to take the picture. This leaves you free to catch the shot quickly, without having to worry about your camera settings.

The program mode chooses settings to give you a compromise between shutter speed and depth of field; it doesn't favor either speed or aperture. This picture has fairly good depth of field; the aperture

setting was about f/8 or f/11. The shutter speed was fast enough to almost completely freeze the motion of the bird's wings—about 1/60 second. When there's more light, the camera uses a smaller aperture and a faster shutter speed; when there's less light, it compromises by opening the aperture and slowing the shutter speed until it reaches a combination that will give you a good exposure.

Check the settings occasionally when you use the program mode to make sure your pictures will come out the way you want them to. When the light is good, as it was here, the camera's aperture/speed compromise will give you good results. But in low light, a camera in the program mode usually won't use shutter speeds slower than 1/30, because that's the slowest speed you can use to hand-hold a shot. Instead, the camera will use large apertures, and this can reduce the depth of field in your picture considerably. Some cameras have a warning light to tell you when the light is too low, so you can use a tripod or take the picture with flash.

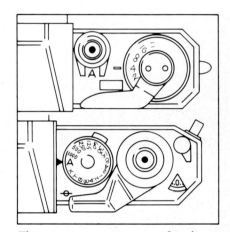

There are two common types of mode selector controls. One type is located next to the shutter speed dial, and indicates the settings for several modes (top); the other is simply an "A" marked on the shutter speed dial (bottom). If the camera has only shutter-preferred and auto modes, the "A" may be on the lens itself.

● To take full advantage of the program mode, set your camera's focus ahead of time so you'll always be ready for a quick shot. First decide how close you want to be to your subjects—say 10 or 12 feet. Then use the depth-of-field scale on the camera lens to set the focus at that distance.

The depth-of-field scale, between the focusing dial and the f-stop ring on the camera lens, has pairs of numbers that indicate f-stops marked on each side of a center line or dot. Set the line so that it lines up with your chosen distance on the focusing ring. As long as you stay at that distance, your subjects will be in focus.

● Light entering the camera lens directly can cause flare in your pictures, so use a lens hood when you photograph outside. When you compose a shot, take note of the angle of the sun; the lens hood should shadow the surface of the lens. Always use a hood that's made for the type of lens you're using, because hoods

sold for other lenses can be ineffective or can cut off the corners of your pictures. If you don't have a lens hood, shield the lens with your hand.

● When the action is fast-paced, you can't count on catching it with the program mode; the shutter-preferred mode is a better choice. If you want to choose which objects you'll have in focus, use the aperture-preferred mode. Use the manual mode when you have time to prepare your shot and you want more control over aperture and shutter speed. All of these modes are explained in this book.

● You'll get the most natural, spontaneous results with candid pictures by approaching your subjects openly but unobtrusively; by acting uneasy or hesitating, you'll draw attention to yourself and lose the unguarded feeling of the moment. When you get close enough to interact, a smile is your best asset.

Be ready to snap a picture quickly when you use the program mode. Keep your camera turned on, with the lens cap off and a hood on the lens. A normal (50mm) or moderate wide-angle (35mm) lens is most useful. Prefocus the camera so you're ready to shoot when you see a good subject.

APERTURE-PREFERRED MODE
The emphasis is up to you

The sharpness of the picture is one of the most important elements of photography, and it can be one of the most creative. When you take a picture, you can choose how much will be in focus. You can decide to make everything in the picture—every leaf and twig, as far back as you can see—sharp. Or you can choose one important subject, and make it the only sharply defined element.

The control that determines focus, or depth of field, is the aperture or f-stop ring. When your camera is set in the aperture-preferred mode, you can choose the aperture you want, for the exact depth of field you want to record. The camera will automatically choose the shutter speed that will give you a good exposure with that f-stop.

The f-stop numbers on the base of the camera lens indicate the size of the aperture, or lens opening. As the f-number increases, the size of the aperture decreases—and the depth of field in the picture increases. At the largest aperture, f/1.4 or f/1.8, only a small part of the picture will be sharp; at the smallest aperture, usually f/22, almost all of the picture will be sharp. This relationship is crucial, because you can use it to give your photographs exactly the effect you want.

In this picture, the photographer used a large aperture to isolate the birds from the trees behind them. The background here would have been distracting; what really matters is the birds themselves. If there had been a whole flock of birds scattered throughout the branches of the tree, a smaller aperture could have been used to bring them all into focus. By changing the aperture, you can photograph one scene in several different ways.

The aperture-preferred mode is most useful where action is not important—where you're more interested in the subject itself than in what it's doing. The uses and effects of small and large apertures are discussed in greater detail later in this book.

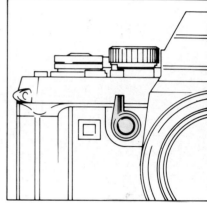

Most cameras have a depth-of-field preview control, located next to or on the lens. Use the depth-of-field preview to see what will be in focus when you take the picture.

Large apertures are very effective where the background is complex; the birds in this photograph are easy to see against the blurred background. Photographed with a small aperture, they would have been lost in the details of the background.

- The depth-of-field preview is very useful when you're using the aperture-preferred mode, because it lets you see how much will be in focus before you take a picture. You can't do this just by looking through the lens, because most cameras don't close down to the aperture you've selected until you press the shutter release. Use the depth-of-field preview to make sure the aperture you've chosen will give you the effect you want.

- When choosing an aperture, remember that f-stop also affects shutter speed—the smaller the aperture, the slower the shutter speed will be. If you use a small aperture such as f/22, but your subject doesn't really call for maximum range of focus, you'll lose shutter speed that you may need to stop action in the picture. Especially in low light, it's often better to limit your depth of field to the most important part of the picture.

- If you limit your depth of field to a particular object, be sure it isn't moving—if it changes position just a little, it could move in and out of focus. This picture was taken with an aperture of f/5.6 or f/8 with a telephoto lens, giving the photographer just enough depth of field to keep the birds sharp without bringing the background into focus.

- If you don't have an aperture-preferred mode on your camera, you can still choose the aperture you need to get the effect you want. If you have a shutter-preferred automatic camera, adjust the shutter speed until you get the right aperture; watch the f-stop indicator through the viewfinder. If you have a manual camera, set the f-stop and adjust the shutter speed until you have a correct exposure reading. You can't choose the aperture you want when your camera is in the program mode.

SHUTTER-PREFERRED MODE
Catch the action, show the motion

One of the most exciting things about photography is that it expresses a feeling of time; it tells us not just what things look like, but how they move and change. You can use your camera to isolate one instant of an action, or to record the continuous motion that occurs over time. Your eye perceives motion in only one way, but the camera can record it in many ways.

The shutter-preferred mode lets you decide how to express motion in your photographs. Unlike the program mode, which balances aperture and shutter speed to give you a compromise, the shutter-preferred mode lets you choose the precise amount of time that will be recorded in the picture. The camera automatically chooses the aperture that will give you a good exposure at this setting.

The depth of field your pictures will have in this mode depends on the shutter speed you choose—the higher the shutter speed, the larger the aperture, and the smaller the area that will be in focus. For this reason, the shutter-preferred mode is most useful when depth of field is not as important as motion—when the background doesn't matter, or you're willing to sacrifice some background detail to capture an instant. In this picture, stopping the action was the only thing that mattered; if the skiers weren't in sharp focus, the effect of the picture would be lost. The shutter-preferred mode is the ideal choice for fast-action sports.

The numbers marked on the shutter speed dial represent seconds and fractions of seconds. The slowest speed is usually 1 (1 second), and the fastest is 500 (1/500 second) or 1000 (1/1000 second). You can stop action at speeds as low as 1/60; you can hold your camera steady for up to 1/30 second. At speeds of 1/500 and 1/1000 second, you can stop the motion of almost any moving object—and with exposures of ½ second, 1 second, or longer, you can take pictures in dim light and record movement over a period of time. The uses and effects of both fast and slow shutter speeds are discussed later in this book.

● It isn't always necessary to stop action to take a good picture. In a fast-action picture, there may be several rates of motion; you can freeze them all or choose to let some parts of the picture blur. Photograph your subject at an even slower speed and you can blur your image so that streaks of color extend across the picture. This effect can be very exciting, and gives you more of a feeling of speed than stopping the motion altogether. Later sections of this book tell you how to freeze or blur motion effectively.

● When deciding which shutter speed to use, remember that shutter speed will also affect depth of field—there's no advantage to using a faster speed than you need. High-speed films are best when you want to freeze motion; they let you use faster shutter speeds without sacrificing depth of field. This picture was taken with a shutter speed of 1/500, with ISO/ASA 200 film. An aperture of f/8 let the photographer keep both skiers in focus.

● If you don't have a shutter-preferred mode on your camera, you can still choose the shutter speed you need to catch or blur motion. If you have an aperture-preferred automatic camera, adjust the aperture until you get the shutter speed you need; you can usually do this by watching the change in shutter speed through the viewfinder. If you have a manual camera, set the speed and adjust the aperture until you have a correct exposure reading. You can't choose the shutter speed you want when your camera is in the program mode.

● If your film speed is not fast enough or there isn't enough light to let you use a fast shutter speed, you can keep your subject in relative focus by following it across your field of view as it passes by. This technique is called panning, and is discussed in a later section.

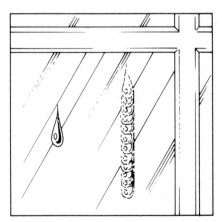

By varying your shutter speed, you can either stop action or record movement. A drop of water, for example, will be sharply recorded with a shutter speed of 1/250 second (left). With a shutter speed of 1 second (right), the movement of the drop will be recorded, and the image will be blurred into a flow.

MANUAL MODE
Take control for perfect pictures

Today's automatic cameras make picture-taking fast and simple, and in most situations, they can give you great results. But sometimes it's important to make exposure decisions yourself—when depth of field and shutter speed are both important; when the light is tricky and your camera meter can't adjust; or when you're taking close-ups.

In this picture, the photographer used the manual mode to get both depth of field and a fast shutter speed. Correct exposure for any picture is a compromise between shutter speed and f-stop, and all the other modes of an automatic camera make the compromise for you—the program mode gives you least control; the shutter- and aperture-preferred modes let you choose only one of these important settings. By using the manual mode, you can control both f-stop and shutter speed, to get exactly the picture you want—every time.

To use the manual mode, you have to decide how you want the picture to look, and then set the f-stop and shutter speed in a combination that will give you the right depth of field and the right exposure time. This combination of settings must also give you a correct exposure.

To get the right exposure, look at the meter exposure indicator in the viewfinder of your camera. This is usually a needle with a plus (+) sign above it and a minus (−) sign below it. When you turn the meter on, the needle will register in the plus range if you need less light, in the minus range if you need more. The exposure is correct when the needle falls in the middle.

To give the film more light, you can either use a larger aperture or use a slower shutter speed; to give the film less light, you can either use a smaller aperture or increase the shutter speed. The advantage of this mode is that you choose the compromise, not the camera. By balancing the factors of speed and aperture, you can make sure your camera gives you the best possible exposure in even the most demanding picture-taking situation.

This photograph depends on both depth of field and shutter speed; a slight breeze was moving the branches, and a small aperture was needed to record the depth of the foliage. The photographer chose a compromise—an aperture of f/8 or f/11, for fairly good depth of field, and a shutter speed of 1/60, showing only slight movement in some parts of the foliage.

● The manual mode is ideal for close-ups, where automatic modes may not be able to make the fine adjustments needed to give you a sharp, well-exposed picture. This is also a good mode to use when your subject is strongly backlighted or there is extreme contrast in the picture, and you can't use the exposure compensation control or the exposure memory lock. In both cases, the automatic modes of your camera might not give you the pictures you want. The exposure compensation control and the exposure memory lock are discussed later in this book.

● To choose the right camera settings where both depth of field and speed are important, first set your aperture; start with f/16 or f/22. Then adjust the shutter speed dial until your camera meter indicates a correct exposure; this will vary with the light and with the speed of your film. If there isn't enough light to let you use as fast a shutter speed as you want—to stop the motion of leaves moving in a breeze, for example, you need a shutter speed of at least 1/60 second—change your aperture setting to one f-stop larger, and try again. The manual mode will let you experiment with different combinations of f-stop and shutter speed until you get the best compromise possible.

● The manual mode can also be used to advantage when you want to favor either depth of field or shutter speed. In this mode, you can choose a small aperture for great depth of field or use a large aperture to emphasize one part of the picture; you can use a fast shutter speed to stop action or a very slow one to blur a moving subject. Use this mode to learn how f-stop and shutter speed work together, and see what effects you can get by trying different combinations. You'll pick up knowledge that will help you take better pictures in any camera mode.

EXPOSURE COMPENSATION
Use uneven light to your advantage

Sometimes, when the light is less than perfect, you can't rely on your camera's exposure meter to read the scene accurately. This picture, with a strong light behind the little girls, shows one of those times. If the photographer had simply trusted his camera meter, the picture would have been underexposed, with the girls' faces lost in shadow and their hair even more brightly haloed. To get the detail and capture the mood of this picture, the photographer had to change the camera's perception of the light.

The exposure compensation control is made for situations like this, where uneven or high-contrast light makes it hard to get an accurate exposure reading. You can use this control to get perfectly exposed photographs when there's too much or too little contrast in the scene for a normal meter reading—when your subject is all bright or all dark, with little contrast; when the background lighting is very different from the light on your subject; or whenever there's extreme contrast.

The exposure compensation control can be used to add light to your subject, as in this picture. It can also be used to decrease the light on your subject. If the little girls were lit from the front, and were standing in front of a large dark background, the camera meter would have overexposed their faces. Compensation settings from +2 (add light) to −2 (subtract light) let you correct the exposure as much or as little as the light demands. This picture was taken with the exposure compensation dial set at +1.

The exposure compensation control isn't the only way to cope with tricky lighting situations—you can also change your ISO/ASA setting, or use the exposure memory lock, discussed in the following section. But the exposure compensation control is the easiest way to meet the challenge. You can use it for a series of pictures when the light isn't changing, and when your subjects are unaware of you or moving around. Here, the photographer would have missed this affectionate moment if he hadn't been able to take a fast shot.

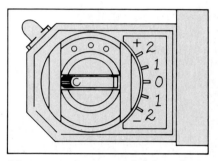

Most exposure compensation controls are part of the ISO/ASA dial on the camera. The numbers on the right mark where you should place the indicator to choose your exposure compensation for more or less light on your subject.

Use the exposure compensation control in any situation where there's a strong backlight and you don't want your pictures to record a silhouette. This control is especially useful when you're photographing people, and their expressions and spontaneous interaction are important.

● There are a few general rules for using the exposure compensation control. If the background is dark and your subject is light, set the dial on −1; or, when the background is very dark, −1½. If the background is light and your subject is dark, as in this picture, set the dial on +1; or, if there's a very strong backlight, +1½. Use +2 when the sun is directly behind your subject; use −2 where there's extreme contrast between a small bright subject and a large dark background.

● Some exposure compensation controls use the numbers ¼, ½, 1X, 2, and 4 on the dial. These are simply another way of indicating the same compensation. The ¼ is the same as −2, and ½ is the same as −1; both decrease the light on your subject. 1X equals 0—no correction. And 2 and 4 are the same as +1 and +2; both increase the light on your subject.

● When taking color slides, you can give your pictures extra color and richness by setting your exposure compensation control at −¼. If the dial doesn't show this setting, estimate it. Always point the camera away from the sky to take your light reading.

● You can keep the exposure compensation at the setting you need for an entire series of photographs, but don't make the costly mistake of forgetting it's on. Always remember to turn the dial back to 0 as soon as you finish shooting or your lighting situation returns to normal.

● When photographing at high altitudes, you can use the exposure compensation control to adjust for the increase in brightness that occurs. Set the dial at −⅓ when you're just a few thousand feet above sea level, and change the setting to −½ as the altitude increases. Use −1 in extremely high altitudes.

THE EXPOSURE MEMORY LOCK
Move close to read the light

The brilliant light that can give your pictures a special feeling can also be very hard to photograph. The sun is an important part of this picture; it creates a halo around the woman and the horse, and emphasizes the cool shade of the tree they're standing under. But if the photographer had relied on his camera meter to take this picture, it would have been underexposed, because the intense light of the background would have dominated the exposure reading.

In any situation where there's this much contrast between the brightness of the subject and the brightness of the background, you'll get the best results by taking an exposure reading from your subject, without including the background. The control that lets you do this is the exposure memory lock.

The exposure memory lock is a button or lever that locks the camera's exposure controls at a particular setting, to let you compensate for extreme contrast in the picture. It is most useful for single pictures, when your subject isn't moving and you have the time to get close. To get this picture, the photographer moved in to his subjects until the woman's face filled the viewfinder. He took his exposure reading directly from her face, and engaged the exposure memory lock to hold those settings. Then he stepped back and took the picture.

The exposure memory lock is the most precise way you can compensate for extreme lighting contrast. Unlike the exposure compensation control, it doesn't rely on an overall reading to make a correction. Instead, it gives you an actual exposure reading—the exposure that will give you the best possible picture of your subject, as if the background didn't exist. This means that you can choose the part of the picture that's most important and make sure that that area is perfectly exposed. The background in this picture was washed out to a featureless brightness, but the woman's face, where the photographer locked in his exposure settings, is warm and natural-looking.

Sometimes the exposure memory lock is located on the camera's mode selector. This one is on the top right side of the camera, next to the film advance lever and the shutter release button.

If the woman and the horse in this picture were standing in front of an open barn door, the contrast would be reversed, with a light subject against a dark background. The exposure memory lock would still be needed for a correct exposure reading; the woman's face would still be the most important element.

● Whenever you're photographing people, the skin tones are the most important area in the picture. To make sure that faces have maximum detail and natural-looking skin tones, move close enough to fill the frame of your viewfinder with your subject's face, and use your exposure memory lock to hold those exposure settings while you step back to compose and shoot your picture.

● If you can't get close enough to take a meter reading directly from your subject's skin, hold your own hand in the same light, and take your exposure reading from that. If your subject's skin tones are much lighter than yours, use an exposure of half an f-stop less than the camera meter indicates; if her skin is much darker, use an exposure of half an f-stop more.

● The exposure memory lock is very useful on overcast days, when your subject is positioned against the gray sky. In this case, the all-gray sky is the brightest part of your picture, and if your picture includes a large sky area, an overall exposure reading will underexpose your subject. By taking your reading directly from your subject, you'll expose for the subject and not the sky.

● If your camera meter has a spot-reading mode, take advantage of it when you use the exposure memory lock. Because this type of metering reads only the light at the center of the frame, you can use it with the memory lock to pinpoint your exposure reading to the exact area that's most important in the picture.

● Exposure memory locks vary, so check your camera manual to see how this control works on your camera. If you don't have an exposure memory lock, use your camera in the manual mode. Take a reading from your subject and then compose and shoot the picture; the camera will not change your exposure settings.

SILHOUETTES
Use light and form for dramatic effect

Few special effects in photography are easier to achieve than the silhouette. A thoughtfully planned lighting situation can give you a sensitive portrait, enhance an already spectacular natural scene, emphasize something special about your subject, or simply create an unusual effect. This picture shows more than the usual view of the Eiffel Tower. It shows the landmark from a different perspective—we become more aware of its shape and its intricate construction.

The key to creating a silhouette is simple: be sure your light source is behind your subject, so that it outlines the subject's shape against a bright background, yet remains hidden. The light that creates this silhouette is the setting sun; the photographer stood under the tower, and chose his camera angle to hide the sun. This natural backlighting is easiest to take advantage of at sunset and sunrise, when the sun is near the horizon and its light is less intense. In this picture, the darkening evening sky provides the perfect background for the framework of the tower.

There are several ways to get the right exposure when you photograph a silhouette. The easiest way is to take your exposure reading from the lighted background, without including the sun or other light source. Set your camera in the manual mode or use the exposure memory lock to set this exposure; then compose the picture and shoot. Your camera will expose the film for the bright background, and your subject will be underexposed, with little or no detail in the foreground.

Another way to get the same effect is to take a reading from the shadowed side of your subject, and then reduce your exposure two f-stops from this reading. Or you can take a reading from a similarly lighted scene, including the sky, and then reduce your exposure one f-stop. You can also vary the effect of the picture by using one f-stop more exposure to bring out more detail in the silhouetted object or person; or you can use one f-stop less exposure to completely eliminate details from the silhouetted shape.

- You can never be sure exactly how a silhouette will come out in the final picture, so it's a good idea to bracket your shots. Take one picture at the exposure you've chosen for the effect you want—for example, f/11 at 1/60 second. Then, by changing the shutter speed, take two more pictures with one stop more and one stop less exposure—f/11 at 1/30 second and f/11 at 1/125 second. This way, you'll be sure to get at least one picture that shows the effect you want to create, and you won't lose depth of field.

- When you take an exposure reading directly from a bright background, be sure you don't include the sun in the reading. Never look directly at the sun, or point your camera directly at it; its intense glare may dazzle your camera meter and give you a false reading, and could damage your eyes. If you think the meter may have been dazzled by the sun, let it recover for a few minutes before you take the picture.

- There are endless possibilities for creating silhouettes. Indoors, you can ask your subjects to pose in front of a crackling fire, a brightly lit window, a table lamp, or any other common light source. Outdoors, you can use street lamps, floodlights, or the sparkling highlights on water to photograph silhouettes.

- When shooting silhouettes at night or in a dimly lit room, use a tripod or other steady base to hold the camera still. Street lamps and sunlit windows don't provide much light, even when you're using high-speed film, and your scene will probably require longer exposure times than you can achieve by hand-holding the camera.

To photograph a silhouette, position yourself between your subject and your light source, as this photographer has done with the Eiffel Tower. The light source—here, the sun—should always be directly behind the object you want to silhouette. Train yourself to pick out silhouettes wherever there's a strong source of light.

MULTIPLE EXPOSURES
Repetition creates the impact

Most pictures consist of one image on a single frame of film—and most cameras are equipped with controls to prevent accidental double exposures. But you can also get good pictures by intentionally putting more than one image on a frame—to create the illusion of movement, or numbers, or changing moods, while still keeping your subject in sharp focus. Multiple exposures can also be used to make scenes that play tricks on the eye, or to add humor and imagination to otherwise ordinary pictures.

In this picture, the photographer used multiple images to create a feeling of motion. He could have used a single exposure to take the picture, but capturing the boy's motion would have required a slow shutter speed. This would have blurred the image, creating a picture with a very different effect. Instead, by taking three sharp pictures of the boy on the same frame, he caught the motion without blurring either boy or bicycle.

Effective multiple exposures take some planning. When you make two or more exposures on the same frame, you're exposing the film to light two or more times—and if you don't allow for this, your pictures may be overexposed. There are no exact rules for exposing multiple images, but there are some general guidelines. Where the background is dark, as in this picture, the important part of the picture—the boy—is not competing with another bright subject, so no exposure compensation is necessary. Where both the subject and the background are bright, you must adjust your camera settings to reduce the exposure to each image.

Deciding how to adjust your camera settings can be tricky, because your subject may have several different colors. For the best results, decide what's most important in the picture, and expose for that. In this picture, the boy's head and body and the red frame of the bicycle are most important, and they are correctly exposed. The boy's feet, positioned against a strip of light background at the bottom of the frame, are in the least important area of the picture, and are overexposed.

To get the correct exposure for a multiple image, decide which part of the picture is most important, and expose for that. In this picture, the boy's head and body are most important, and they're correctly exposed. The wheels and feet overlap, so they're exposed twice; the background at the bottom of the picture, with three exposures, is washed out.

● The effectiveness of a multiple image depends on the sharpness of the individual images, so use a fast shutter speed to keep your subject clearly defined. The shutter speed you need to freeze motion depends on the speed and direction of the motion and on how close you are to your subject; this is discussed later, in the section on freezing motion. You can also use electronic flash to make multiple exposures; the uses and effects of flash are discussed in later sections.

● When photographing a light subject against a light background, adjust your camera settings so that each exposure gets only a fraction of the total exposure needed. Place the number 1 over the number of exposures you intend to make, and allow each image that much of the total. For two exposures, you need only ½ as much light; use one f-stop less exposure for each image. For three images, stop down 1½ stops for each exposure; for four, stop down two stops; and so on. To make sure you get the results you want, first use the exposure you think is correct; then shoot the sequence twice more, using one f-stop more and one f-stop less exposure.

● Check your camera manual to see if your camera can be used to take multiple exposures. If you can't advance the shutter without advancing the film, you can rewind the film manually—one frame equals approximately three-quarters to one revolution on your rewind dial. This method doesn't guarantee results, because it's difficult to line the pictures up exactly.

● Another way to take multiple exposures is to take a whole roll of pictures, recording exactly what is on each frame, and then use the same roll of film again to make the second exposure. This technique is sometimes used in commercial photography. Mark a line on the film when you put it in the camera the first time, and use this to start the film in the same place the second time.

FRAMING AND COMPOSITION
Pay attention to what you see

The camera's viewfinder gives you vital information for taking pictures. In it, you see exactly the picture you'll have when you press the shutter release. You also see exposure information.

With all the information it gives you, the viewfinder's most important function is to help you compose the picture. Composition is an essential part of photography, because the camera—unlike the human eye—cannot distinguish between what's important and what's not; it simply records everything it sees. The key to good composition is to look at the image in the viewfinder—and to pay attention to everything you see.

There are no strict rules for composing a picture, but there are some guidelines. Look at the position and relative size of your subject, and at the objects around it—if your subject takes up only a quarter of the frame, it will measure only about an inch high in a 3½ x 5-inch print. Look for the most striking shape or color in your image—a strong outline, a rich texture, an intricate detail—and organize the rest of the picture around it. Look at the background, and make sure your subject stands out from it—or, if you want it to blend, make sure you like the effect.

The shape of your subject, and the way it fits within the frame, are also important. Try both horizontal and vertical framings to see which one works better. Don't be afraid to try different angles of view—lie down, squat, climb a ladder. Walk around and look at your subject until you find the best approach, and then move close enough so that your subject fills the frame of the viewfinder. Leave unimportant and distracting elements out of the picture, and watch the edges of the frame—by cutting off objects at the edges, you emphasize their importance and weaken the impact of the picture.

All of these details contribute to good composition, whether you're photographing people or places, animals or objects. In any picture-taking situation, you can improve your pictures by learning to see through the camera's eye.

If this picture were framed horizontally, it would include distracting background elements at the sides, and the man's body would be cut off abruptly. If the photographer had not filled the frame with his subject, the man would be too small in the picture, and too much meaningless background would be included.

- If your camera is manual, the viewfinder probably shows a needle that indicates whether you need more or less light to take a picture. If you have an automatic camera, you'll see the shutter speed the camera is set for, the f-stop setting, or both. Some cameras even have indicators to tell you what mode the camera is in and whether the picture is in focus. Pay attention to all this information, and use it to get the best possible exposure.

- Pictures of people, and especially portraits, require special attention. Keep your subject large, and keep his head high in the frame. Hold the camera at eye level. Placing your subject slightly off center, as this photographer did, can give the picture a good sense of balance. Be sure to include enough of your subject's body—hands especially can add a great deal of meaning to the picture. Frame the picture carefully to be sure the background doesn't interfere with the person.

- Make sure the camera is level when you photograph a landscape. Buildings and trees should line up with the vertical sides of the frame, and if your picture includes the horizon, make sure it's straight. You can eliminate the horizon from scenic pictures by pointing the camera slightly up, so that only sky appears in the frame, or slightly down, so that only the ground appears. If you photograph a person against the horizon, watch the line; it may cut through his head or neck.

- When your subject's size isn't apparent, include an indicator of scale—a person or any clearly recognizable object—to put the picture into perspective. Use your depth-of-field preview to see exactly how much of the picture is in focus.

The mistakes in composition that can ruin your pictures can also give you funny and unusual results, with surrealistic effects created by careful positioning. Experiment to see how you can use these effects for fun.

LIGHT, DARK, AND COLOR
Use contrast to create meaning

Light and color can set a mood, define a shape, and reveal depth and texture so vividly in a photograph that you want to reach out and touch it. You can use light and color to create any effect you like in your pictures—all you have to do is look.

There are three important elements in every color photograph: the subject itself, the light, and the color. Look at this picture of a single purple flower against vivid green lily pads. The bright pads stand out strongly against the dark water, and the shadow of the flower makes the color contrast even more effective. Both kinds of contrast contribute to the picture's impact.

The contrast between light and dark gives meaning to what we see, and it can either clarify or cause confusion in your pictures. In strong direct light, shadows can enhance your subject or obscure essential parts of the picture, add texture or flatten it. In uniform light, as on an overcast day, shadows disappear, and contrast is less noticeable. Colors are richest and most intense in soft light, or when the light is behind you.

Look for the effect of shadows when you compose your pictures. Photograph when the light will give you the effect you want—shadows are longest and most visually important when the sun is low; when the sun is directly overhead, the shadows disappear. You can see the effect of light and shadow in the scene by squinting.

The colors in a picture can be used in several ways—to create contrast and make your subject stand out against the background, or to create an image in which shape and texture are more important than color. Some colors—reds, oranges, and yellows—are warm and vibrant, and will pop out of the picture; others—cool colors like blue and green, and neutral tones like brown and gray—seem to recede. Pay attention to the colors and color relationships in the scene when you compose your pictures; if you look for subtle or striking color in the things around you, you'll start to see good photographs before you take them.

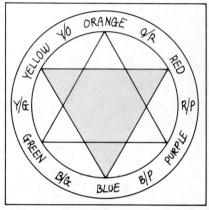

The color wheel shows the relationships among colors. Primary colors are those marked on the shaded triangle; secondary colors are marked on the unshaded triangle. Colors opposite each other are called complementary colors.

● For maximum color contrast in your pictures, watch for combinations of warm and cool colors, or of complementary colors—pink and green, blue and yellow, red and blue-green. The primary colors also work well together. Remember that warm colors will pop out of the picture—if you pose a cool-color subject against a warm-color background, your subject will recede and the background will become the dominant element.

● You don't have to use strong contrasts to get good pictures. Try photographing a subject with one predominant color against a neutral background—black, white, or any neutral tone. You can also restrict the colors in the picture to muted, subtle shades—browns, ochers, and other earth tones—to get a very rich, calm scene.

● Even a gray day can give you photographs with rich, vibrant colors, but compose your pictures to include as little gray sky as possible. Try shooting pictures from a high angle, so that the sky won't dominate the colors in the scene.

● The subject is usually important, but you can also make light and color the primary elements in the picture, by using them to create shapes or textures. When you take a picture to silhouette an object, its shape—and the contrast between light and dark—is most important. You can also focus on abstract shapes or textures formed by areas of strongly contrasting or coordinating colors.

Shadows can define the shape of your subject or change it entirely. They can also create a whole new form in the picture, as they do in this sketch of the shadows cast by a fence. Look for interesting shadows whenever the sun is low in the sky or your subject is strongly side-lighted.

THE NORMAL LENS
Take the picture as you see it

The lens you use to take a photograph has a significant effect on the way the picture will look. Usually, although you may want other lenses for special projects, you'll find that the most versatile lens you have is the one that came with your camera—the normal lens, usually a 50mm.

This colorful picture was a perfect subject for the normal lens. The photographer wanted to show this scene the way he saw it, so that the size of the hot-air balloon was apparent—and the normal lens gives you an image with almost the same apparent size you see. It gives you the widest range of working distances, and the best compromise between the ability to record detail at those distances and the amount of the scene you can take in.

The normal lens is good for taking pictures of groups of people involved in outdoor activities, and for scenic shots—especially when there are buildings in the picture—that include a good portion of the scene around you. It can give you good results in most everyday picture-taking situations.

The image you see in the viewfinder when you take a picture depends on the focal length of the lens you're using. With the normal (50mm) lens, it's close to what you see without the camera. When you use a lens with a longer focal length—a telephoto—you see less of the scene; when you use a lens with a shorter focal length—a wide-angle—you see more. Both of these lenses change the image you see by bringing you closer or farther away from your subject, making the picture area smaller or larger than what you see. To record the scene as it appears to you, you have to use a normal lens.

In this picture the photographer used the normal lens to show the perspective of the scene—its depth and distance, illustrated by the sizes of nearby and distant objects. The people give us a point of reference. By including both the people walking across the balloon and the people working on the basket in the distance, the photographer made the wide expanse of bright color even more striking.

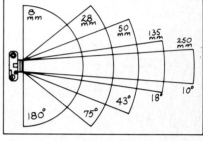

This diagram shows the relative angles of view of common lenses. Notice that the smallest size lens, or shortest, gives you the greatest angle of view; the longest lens gives you the most limited.

The photographer could have used a telephoto lens (smaller frame) to focus more closely on the people in the foreground of this picture, or a wide-angle lens (larger frame) to include more of the scene. But only the normal lens could record the scene as he actually saw it.

● The normal lens is built with a larger maximum aperture than most other lenses, so you can let in more light with a 50mm lens than you can with a 28mm or a 300mm—a real advantage in low light. You can carry it easily and hand-hold it at shutter speeds as slow as 1/30 second.

● The normal lens gives you the best compromise between breadth and depth of field, but it can't always give you the effect you want. If you find you have too much or too little in the picture, and you can't change position for a better framing, try using another lens—a longer lens to cover a smaller area, a shorter lens to cover a wider area. The best lens is one that lets you fill the frame of the viewfinder with your subject.

● The image you'll record in your pictures depends on the angle of view of the lens—the angle measured from the center of the lens and out in all directions from the front of the camera. The smaller the focal length of the lens, the wider the angle of view it will record on film. A wide-angle lens gives you a wide angle of view; use it for shots where you want to include as much of the scene as possible. A telephoto lens gives you a limited angle of view; use it where you want to isolate your subject and magnify it for greater detail.

● Zoom lenses are lenses that can be adjusted to vary their focal length; they allow you to change your angle of view without changing the lens on your camera. They're available in many focal length ranges, and usually have a zoom ratio of 2:1 or 3:1—the longest focal length is two or three times greater than the shortest. Common zoom ranges are 35mm to 85mm, 70mm to 200mm, and 200mm to 600mm.

TELEPHOTO LENSES
Emphasize the essentials

If you're observant, you can find good pictures everywhere—in patterns of light and color, in details of a larger scene, in appealing faces and interesting objects. You can capture these pictures, as the photographer here captured the reflections of the line of boats, with telephoto lenses.

Telephoto lenses are longer than the normal (50mm) lens—usually from 85mm to 1000mm. They give you a narrower angle of view, and a shallower depth of field—the longer the lens, the more extreme the results. The narrow viewing angle of a telephoto lens isolates your subject, and magnifies it in the frame of the picture. The lens's shallow depth of field blurs the background, emphasizing your subject even more.

You can use these characteristics to isolate one detail of a larger scene, as this photographer did. You can also use a telephoto to get close to a subject that's unreachable—like a wild animal—or to stay at a distance from a subject you don't want to distract, like a child playing. In both cases, you can use the telephoto's shallow depth of field to eliminate meaningless background details.

Telephoto lenses have one other noticeable effect: they compress the perspective of the scene, so that subjects at varying distances from the camera seem to be piled up very close to each other. You can use this effect to bring distant objects close to nearby ones—to stack distant buildings against closer ones, for instance, to emphasize the crowded feeling of a city.

Telephoto lenses are ideal for any situation where you want to get closer to your subject—for sports photography, candid shots, and scenic pictures where your main point of interest is a good distance away from you. They're also very good for portrait photography. With a normal (50mm) lens, you can't eliminate background details unless you get very close to your subject, and this can cause distortion in the picture. With an 85mm to 105mm telephoto lens, you can get close to your subject without including a lot of background, with no distortion.

This group of boats was a small part of a larger scene; the photographer used a telephoto lens to get close. With a normal (50mm) lens, he couldn't have isolated this detail.

● Telephoto lenses are heavy, and they magnify any slight shakiness during a handheld shot. To prevent blurring, use a shutter speed at least as fast as the length of the lens—1/125 second with a 105mm lens, 1/250 second with a 200mm lens, and so on. Where there isn't enough light to use a fast shutter speed, use a tripod and a cable release to make sure your pictures are sharp.

● Because a telephoto lens magnifies your subject, a moving subject will move across the frame of the picture much more quickly than with a normal (50mm) lens, and you'll need a much faster shutter speed to stop the action. Image size increases in direct proportion to lens length. A 200mm lens records an object four times larger than a 50mm lens does; the object will move across the frame four times faster, and you'll need a shutter speed four times faster to stop it.

● Certain telephoto lenses are recommended for specific shooting situations. An 85mm to 135mm lens is good for both portraits and scenic shots; a 135mm to 300mm lens is better for sports. To get close to wildlife, you need a lens with a focal length of 500mm to 1000mm.

● Telephoto zoom lenses are very useful, because they let you take several different pictures from one camera position, both focusing on details and recording a wider angle of view. You can also use a telephoto zoom—a 70mm to 200mm lens works well—to take informal portraits; have your subject walk toward you, and shoot at different focal lengths as he approaches. The exposure you need will change as you zoom in on your subject; if you're using the manual mode of your camera, be sure to take a new exposure reading at each focal length.

If you don't have a tripod with you, use any solid support to steady a telephoto lens—a piling, a wall, even the top of a parked car. Hold the lens barrel steady with your hand while you take the picture.

WIDE-ANGLE LENSES
Take a wider look at the world

Not every picture has to be one your eye could focus. Sometimes you may want to emphasize one part of the picture, like the beer mug in this photograph of a bartender. Sometimes you may need a wider angle of view to take in more of the scene than you can get with a normal lens—when you're photographing a group of people, for instance. And sometimes, when you're aiming for a special effect, you may want to distort your subject, as the photographer of this cityscape has done. You can do all of these things with wide-angle lenses.

Wide-angle lenses are shorter than the normal (50mm) lens. They give you a much wider angle of view—about twice as wide as the normal lens provides—so you can get close to your subject and still take in all of it, instead of having to limit your picture to one object. Wide-angle lenses also give you excellent depth of field, so that more of the picture will be in focus than with a normal lens.

The shorter the lens you use, the more extreme these effects will be, and the more noticeably your subject will be distorted.

Very short lenses, with a focal length of 21mm or less, record scenes very differently from the way you see them; they're good only where you want special effects. Moderate wide-angles, with a focal length of 24mm to 35mm, are the most practical of the short lenses; you can use them to get effects like the bartender's mug and to shoot pictures that aren't noticeably distorted. A moderate wide-angle is essential for group photography, and it's also good for interior and city shots.

A more extreme type of wide-angle is the fisheye lens, used to take this severely distorted shot of a city street. Fisheye lenses, while they are considered wide-angles, are built with a differently shaped lens; the image they produce appears spherical. A fisheye can have a wider angle of view than any other lens, and produces pictures with a very distinctive kind of distortion.

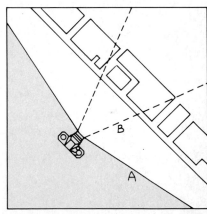

With a wide-angle lens, you can get very close to your subject and still include his surroundings in the picture. Taken with a normal lens (outline A), this picture would show only the beer mug, instead of the entire scene (outline B).

A fisheye lens takes in an extreme angle of view (outline A), and produces the effect of being part of the picture. A normal lens (outline B) would take in only the front of one or two buildings at the same distance.

● Wide-angle lenses make distant objects look smaller, and distances between objects look greater. Because of their extreme depth of field, wide-angles let you bring everything in the picture into focus at small apertures, from directly in front of the camera to infinity. This is particularly good in group pictures where you want everyone's face to be clearly defined.

● When you photograph interior scenes with a wide-angle lens, remember that wide-angles can distort the shape of objects at the edges or corners of the picture. Avoid placing strongly defined vertical elements, like doors or windows, at the edges of the frame; unintended distortion could be disturbing.

● Wide-angle lenses are easy to hand-hold, but they're hard to focus—everything in the picture looks sharp when you look through the lens. To make sure your pictures are focused, use the depth-of-field scale on the lens. Estimate the dis-

tance from the camera to the object you want to focus on, and the range of distances you want in focus. Set the nearest and farthest distances between the pair of numbers that indicate your f-stop depth-of-field scale. As long as you stay at this distance, your subject will be in focus.

● To get the most use from a wide-angle lens, buy one that falls in the 28mm to 35mm range—28mm is a good length to start with. If you don't want to buy a separate lens, you may be able to use a low-cost wide-angle adapter in front of your normal lens. Try the adapter before you buy to be sure it fits your camera.

● Light striking a wide-angle lens can cause flare in your pictures, so always use a lens hood when photographing in bright light. Use a hood made specifically for the wide-angle lens; a hood made for a longer lens will cut off the edges of your pictures.

CLOSE-UPS
Concentrate on the details

Photography takes on a whole new dimension when we turn away from the highly visible world we see and concentrate on smaller, less conspicuous images. This picture of a daisy shows details we wouldn't ordinarily notice—the delicate shades of color in the petals, their velvety texture, and the interesting patterns that make up the flower's black center. The image is completely different from what we usually see.

The easiest way to take close-up pictures is with close-up lenses, supplementary lenses that attach to the front of your normal (50mm) camera lens. Close-up lenses are rated in positive powers: +1, +2, +3, and so on. The larger the number, the more the lens will magnify the image, and the closer you can get to your subject. With a +1 lens, for instance, you can get as close as 20 inches; with a +3, you can get as close as 10 inches.

Composition is important in close-up photography, because you can include only a few elements in the picture. Place your subject carefully within the frame of the picture, and use patterns and shapes creatively to fill the space. The image should be simple, with strong color and maximum clarity, to give you a picture that's both realistic and striking.

The greatest challenge of close-up photography is keeping the picture sharp—the closer you get, the less depth of field you'll have. This problem is intensified by the size of the image in the frame; because the image is large, the slightest movement will be magnified in the picture. This means that both aperture and shutter speed are important.

For the best results with close-ups, set your camera in the manual mode so that you can balance f-stop and shutter speed; the automatic mode can't make the fine adjustments necessary to get a sharp image. Set your camera on a tripod, and use a cable release to minimize camera shake. When you're photographing outdoors, wait for the wind to die down, so you can use the smallest possible aperture to take the picture.

● Soft, diffused light will give you the best color and the most accurate exposure with close-ups. Take your exposure reading from a middle tone in the picture, without including highlights or deep shadows. A slow or medium film (ISO/ASA 64 or less) will give you the best detail and color.

● If you can't get close enough to your subject, use a telephoto lens to fill the frame of the viewfinder. To magnify the image even more, you can also put a close-up lens on your telephoto lens.

● Where your depth of field is very limited, focus on the most important area or detail in the picture, the one that would lose the most meaning if it were out of focus. This is called critical focus, and is discussed in more detail in a separate section.

● When the existing light is inadequate, you can use flash to add light and bring out more detail. A ring flash, which attaches to the lens of your camera, is best for soft, even light throughout the picture; a standard flash can create unwanted shadows.

● Professional photographers use bellows systems and extension tubes to take close-up photographs. These are very precise and require a lot of calculation to adjust for exposure. If you plan to do a lot of close-up work, consider investing in a macro lens, a type of lens that's specially designed for close-ups. Macro lenses are commonly available in focal lengths of 50mm and 105mm.

To set up a close-up photograph outdoors, set your camera on a tripod; use a cable release to eliminate camera shake. You can reflect light back into the shadowed areas with a white card.

SMALL APERTURES
Keep the whole picture sharp

When you photograph a scene that has a lot of interesting detail and color, you'll probably want everything in the picture to be in focus. In this picture, the photographer wanted to record maximum clarity and detail in all the flags—all of them contribute equally to the strong diagonal pattern, and together, they give the scene a feeling of great depth. If only a few of the flags were in focus, this would be a much less effective image; the impact of the long line of flags would be gone.

To get this much depth of field, the photographer used a small lens aperture—a large f-number. The highest f-stops on the camera lens—f/16 and f/22—indicate the smallest lens openings, and the smaller the aperture you use, the greater the depth of field your pictures will have. By learning to apply this principle, you can control the sharpness of every object in your pictures.

This scene was photographed at an aperture of f/16 or f/22. If the photographer had used a larger aperture—a smaller f-number—less of the picture would be in focus. At an aperture of f/2.8, only one flag would be sharp; the rest would be progressively more blurred as their distance from the point of focus increased.

With a normal (50mm) lens, apertures of f/16 and f/22 will record sharpness throughout the scene. At f/11 or f/8, the depth of field will be less, but not significantly. At aperture settings of f/5.6 and f/4, you can't expect sharpness in depth; objects in front of your subject and behind it will be out of focus. And at apertures of f/2.8 and larger, only the object you focus on will be sharp.

When great depth of field is an important element in the scene, as it is here, choose the smallest aperture you can to keep everything in the picture sharp. Remember that you can't tell how much of the picture will be in focus by looking through the lens. Use the camera's depth-of-field preview to be sure you're getting the effect you want.

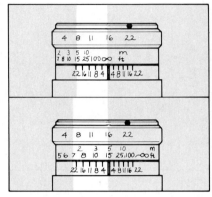

To get maximum depth of field at small apertures, set the center line of the lens depth-of-field scale so that the distance of the farthest object you want focused lines up with the right-hand marking for your aperture setting. In the top sketch, the focus is set at infinity, and sharpness begins at 15 feet from the camera. In the bottom sketch, the focus is set at 15 feet, and sharpness begins at 7 feet.

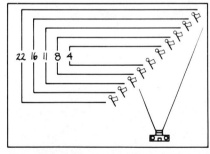

How much of the scene will be sharp in a picture depends on the f-stop you use; the smaller the aperture—the larger the f-number—the greater the depth of field in the picture. The photographer here used an aperture of f/16 to get all the flags sharp.

- To get great depth of field in a picture, set your camera in the aperture-preferred mode, or use the manual mode to set both f-stop and shutter speed. If your camera is a shutter-preferred one, choose the aperture for the picture by adjusting the shutter speed until the camera gives you the aperture you want. Don't use the program mode; the aperture setting you get in this mode is always a compromise.

- At small apertures, you'll have to use slow shutter speeds to get well-exposed pictures. When you choose your f-stop, check to see what shutter speed is necessary at that exposure. At speeds slower than 1/30 second, use a tripod to hold the camera steady.

- When your subject is moving, you'll have to use a fast shutter speed to stop the action. In dim light you may not have enough light to use both a fast shutter speed and a small aperture; in this case, you'll have to use a larger aperture—a smaller f-number—to take the picture. This scene was bright enough so that the photographer could use both a small aperture and a shutter speed fast enough to stop the fluttering of the flags.

- If you can't get the entire picture sharp, try moving away from your subject—the farther away you are, the greater the depth of field will be in the picture. Depth of field is also affected by the focal length of your lens—the greater the focal length, the smaller the depth of field; the smaller the focal length, the greater the depth of field. Telephoto lenses have considerably less depth of field than the normal (50mm) lens, and wide-angle lenses have considerably more. If you want to increase the depth of field in a picture but you can't move back, you can use a wide-angle lens to increase the zone of sharpness in the picture.

LARGE APERTURES
Put the accent where you want it

A good picture doesn't always require that everything in the frame be in focus—sometimes you can get much better results by limiting the depth of field. In this picture, the photographer used a narrow range of focus to emphasize the little girl at the front—to concentrate our attention on her expression, instead of showing her as one of a group of children. By choosing his aperture setting carefully, he kept just enough detail in the other two faces so that we can still identify them and find pleasure in their expressions. The strong appeal of the picture is a result of this selective focusing.

To limit the sharpness of this picture to one important area, the photographer chose a large lens aperture—a small f-number. The lowest f-stops on the camera lens—f/2.8 and f/2—indicate the largest lens openings, and the larger the aperture you use, the smaller the part of your picture that will be in sharp focus. This means that you can use large apertures for pictures where you don't want to show the entire scene—when one part of the picture is more important, as it is here, or when you want to make your subject stand out sharply against the background. This technique is used very often for portraits, for wildlife photographs, and for sports pictures.

This picture was taken with an aperture of about f/5.6, so that the faces in the background wouldn't be completely blurred. Settings of f/4, f/2.8, and f/2 will give you progressively less depth of field; at f/2, the background will be nearly featureless. Because you must choose a particular aperture to focus selectively, set your camera in the aperture-preferred mode for this kind of photography, or use the manual mode to set both f-stop and shutter speed.

To get good pictures with selective focus, you must be able to judge the sharpness you'll get with various f-stops. You can't tell from the image in the viewfinder how much of the scene will be in focus, so use the depth-of-field preview to make sure you have the right aperture for the amount of sharpness you want.

● With a normal (50mm) lens, use an aperture setting of f/4 or f/5.6 to put the background slightly out of focus, while still keeping shapes and features recognizable. To completely blur the background, use an f-stop setting of f/2.8 or f/2.

● With large apertures, you can use fast shutter speeds to get well-exposed pictures, so stopping movement isn't hard. Check to see what shutter speed is required at the aperture you want; it may be considerably faster than a normal setting. If you need a shutter speed of 1/60 second with an aperture of f/8, for instance, a speed of 1/250 will be required with an aperture of f/4.

● The aperture-preferred or manual mode is best for selective focusing, but you can also use the shutter-preferred mode to focus selectively. Adjust the shutter speed until the camera gives you the right aperture for the effect you want —watch the f-stop settings in the viewfinder. Don't use the program mode for pictures where you want to focus selectively; the success of this technique depends on your ability to choose the right settings.

● Selective focus is especially effective when you're using a telephoto lens, because a telephoto gives you less depth of field than the normal (50mm) lens does. This picture was taken with a moderate (135mm) telephoto lens; the two faces behind the little girl look closer to her than they really are. Very long telephoto lenses, 500mm to 1000mm, are popular for wildlife shots, because they isolate the subject completely from the background. Wide-angle lenses are not suitable for selective focusing; their depth of field is usually too great.

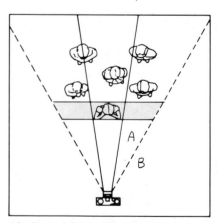

The limited depth of field in this picture (shaded area) separates the little girl from the other two people in the scene, making her the only important subject among the three. The photographer used a telephoto lens for a narrower angle of view (outline A); outline B shows the same scene through a normal (50mm) lens.

SPECIAL FOCUS TECHNIQUES
Record important details sharply

The sharpness of a photograph has a direct bearing on its clarity and impact. Usually it's easy to focus, but there are two situations where getting a sharp picture can be very hard—when your subject is moving so fast you don't have time to focus, and when your depth of field is very limited.

Each of these photographers used a special technique to focus effectively. The technique used to catch the polo pony is called zone focus—the photographer focused at a particular distance and waited for the action to come to that point. The technique used to photograph the cactus is called critical focus; the photographer chose the one part of the subject that was most critical to the meaning of the picture, and focused on that part. In each case, the photographer used a tripod to hold the camera steady, and set his exposure ahead of time.

Zone focus is ideal for photographing fast-paced sports or games, and whenever your subject is moving too fast for you to focus on it. The principle is simple: focus your camera at the point where you want to take the picture—here, the playing field at the point where the pony is—and wait for your subject to come to you. Use as small an aperture—as large an f-number—as you can; the more depth of field you have, the less critical it is to take the picture at one precise instant, and the easier it is to get a sharp picture.

Critical focus is most often used in close-up photography, when speed is not critical and depth of field is very limited. The principle here is to focus on the most interesting part of your subject—the part that best serves as a point of visual impact, or the texture or detail that would lose the most visual meaning if it were blurred. In this picture, the photographer focused on a single row of thorns to establish the form of the cactus.

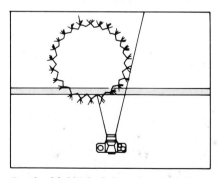

To prepare for a shot that requires zone focus, estimate the point where your subject will give you the best picture, and focus on that point (X). Use your depth-of-field preview to see how much of the area ahead of that point and beyond it (shaded area) will be in focus.

● Use a tripod to photograph with either of these techniques. In a zone-focus situation, set up your camera and frame the area where you want to take the picture; then set your exposure and focus. This lets you concentrate on watching the action. In a critical-focus situation, the camera must be steady to make the most of the picture's limited depth of field. Use a cable release to minimize vibration.

● Since depth of field is crucial, use your depth-of-field preview to see how much of the picture will be in focus. The area that's recorded sharply in your photograph will extend about one-third in front of your point of focus and two-thirds beyond it.

● To stop the action of a fast-paced sport like polo, you'll have to use a fast shutter speed. In this picture, the polo pony was coming toward the photographer at a slight diagonal, so a speed of 1/125 or 1/250 second could catch the action. If the rider had been moving directly across the frame, a higher speed—1/500 or 1/1000 second—would have been needed. To get the shutter speed you need to stop fast action, while still retaining a small aperture, use a fast film, ISO/ASA 200 or higher.

● When you use a telephoto lens as the photographer did to get this picture of the polo pony, zone focus is often the only practical way to get a sharp picture, because it's very hard to get a sharp image when you swing a long lens to follow your subject. Close-up lenses often require the use of critical focus, because they give you a very shallow depth of field.

Depth of field (shaded area) is so shallow in close-ups that you'll have to use critical focus. Focus precisely on the most important part of the picture, and let the rest blur.

FAST SHUTTER SPEEDS
Freeze the action

With a fast shutter speed, you can use your camera to record brief moments that your eyes aren't quick enough to see—to catch drops of water in the air, to capture a great play in a close game, to stop the movements of a running child. From the photo finish to the high-speed scientific image, high-speed photography is always exciting.

The shutter speed you need to stop the movement of your subject depends on three things—how fast it's moving, what direction it's moving in, and how far away from it you are—as well as how much light there is on the scene. Two of these factors—the speed and the direction of your subject—you'll have to estimate. You can vary your distance from your subject to get the results you want, and you can also choose a fast film, ISO/ASA 200 or higher, to make the best use of the available light.

To choose the right shutter speed when you want to stop action, look at the image in the viewfinder, and see how fast it's changing. When you're close to your subject, its image will be large, and it will change quickly. When you're far away, the image will be smaller, and will seem to change more slowly. The image will also change quickly when your subject is moving fast, and when it's moving directly across the scene—a subject that's moving slowly, or one that's coming right at you, is easier to keep in the viewfinder.

You'll need the fastest speeds to stop the action in a scene when it's close to you, moving quickly, directly across the viewfinder. Use a speed of 1/125 second to capture a baby who won't hold still, or conversational gestures; a speed of 1/60 to 1/125 second for a person walking across the frame, 20 feet away; a speed of 1/60 second for a person walking straight toward you. To photograph drops of water in the air, or a person running or riding a bicycle across the frame, 20 feet away, use a shutter speed of 1/1000 second; to stop a person running toward you, use 1/250 or 1/500 second.

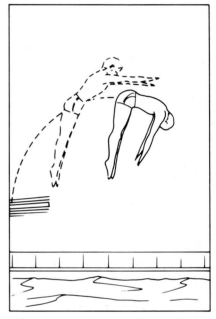

When the action has a peak, as it does when your subject is a diver, anticipate the peak and take the picture just as this split-second pause begins. Here, the outline shows the best moment to shoot.

● Since shutter speed is the crucial setting when you want to stop action, set your camera for shutter-preferred operation; you can also use the manual mode to choose both shutter speed and aperture. If your camera is aperture-preferred, adjust the aperture until you get the right shutter speed. Don't try to freeze motion with your camera in the program mode; this will give you an intermediate shutter speed.

● Fast shutter speeds usually require large apertures, so don't use a faster speed than you need to stop the action, especially in dim light. Set your shutter speed and see what f-stop is required at that speed; use the depth-of-field preview to see how much of the picture will be in focus. Zone focus is often helpful in stopping action. To be sure you get the results you want, take more than one picture—the first at the settings you think you need, and then one or two more at faster or slower speeds.

● When you photograph with a telephoto lens, you'll need faster shutter speeds to stop the action, because the lens brings your subject closer. The shutter speeds given here are calculated for a normal (50mm) lens. To figure the speed you need with a telephoto, multiply by the proportional focal length of the lens you're using. A 200mm lens, for example, is four times longer than a normal (50mm) lens, so you'll need a shutter speed four times faster than with a normal lens. A wide-angle lens can get good results with slower speeds.

● You don't always have to stop the action completely to get a good picture. In many action situations there are several rates of motion, and you can enhance the feeling of the action by blurring some of it. In this picture, the girl's hand is blurred; it was moving faster than the rest of her body. The contrast, and the slight blur of the water drops, add to the sense of action in the scene.

The angle of the action also affects the shutter speed you need. To stop a bicyclist moving directly across the frame 20 feet away, use a shutter speed of 1/1000 second; to stop the same action coming toward you, use 1/250 second. When the bicycle is coming toward you diagonally, you need a speed between these extremes: 1/500 second.

SLOW SHUTTER SPEEDS
Show the flow of the motion

The fluid quality of motion—in a person, an animal, an object, a stream of water—is something that stop-action photography just can't show. In this picture, the photographer could have frozen the boy's pitch in a single pose, but by using a slow shutter speed, he recorded an image that captures the flow of the movement. Shutter speeds slow enough to record motion in time can recreate the excitement of the action you see, and create expressive images that you normally can't see.

The shutter speed you need to blur motion depends on the same factors involved in stopping the action—how fast your subject is moving, what direction it's moving in, and how close to it you are, as well as how much light there is. The closer you are, the more motion you'll record; the faster the movement, the more your picture will blur. The photographer here was standing close enough so that the boy's image fills the frame of the picture; a shutter speed of ¼ second was slow enough to blur his movements. The boy's arms were moving faster than the rest of him, so they are blurred more than any other part of the picture.

This photograph expresses movement in two ways: the photographer used a slow shutter speed to record the boy's movement, and he moved the camera during the exposure to emphasize the feeling of action in the picture. Where you want to blur only your subject, use a tripod to hold the camera steady during the long exposure required to record motion.

The amount of blur your pictures will record is unpredictable, so experiment with a variety of shutter speeds—every picture will be different. To blur the action of children playing, try exposures of 1/15 second or longer; to blur a very fast-moving subject, like a train, 1/60 second may be slow enough. Try shutter speeds of ½ second and 1 second when your subject is a dancer; you can blur fast-flowing water to a smoky mist with a shutter speed of 1 second. To record motion over long periods of time, use your camera to make time exposures, as explained later in this book.

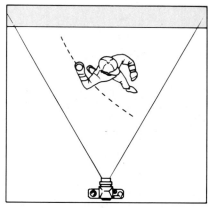

The motion in this picture is most evident where the boy's arms are moving fast across the frame. The black background makes his red sleeves stand out vividly.

● In most cases, you'll have to use a small aperture to get a slow shutter speed, especially where the light is strong. Set your camera in the shutter-preferred mode so that you can choose the shutter speed, or set both shutter speed and aperture manually. If you have an aperture-preferred camera, adjust the aperture until you get the shutter speed you want. Don't use the program mode where you want to record motion; the camera will always tend to freeze the action.

● For the best results, photograph your subject against a dark background; colors won't be recorded as strongly against a light background. Take your exposure reading for the most important color in the picture—here, the boy's arms and body. When you're photographing flowing water, take a reading from the water itself, or use an exposure of ½ f-stop less than your camera meter indicates to retain detail in the water and make the surrounding foliage richer.

● You can hand-hold the camera at speeds as slow as 1/30 second, but for slower speeds, use a tripod to hold the camera steady. If you don't have a tripod with you, use a fence post, a wall, or any other solid support to steady the camera. You can hand-hold the camera at shutter speeds up to four times slower by bracing yourself against a solid object. Brace your elbows against your body, relax, and take a deep breath; let it out slowly and then release the shutter.

● You can also record movement in a scene by moving your camera—as this photographer did—or by moving the camera to follow your subject's action, called panning. Panning is discussed later in this book. Another way to get an effect of movement is to use a zoom lens on your camera, and to zoom the lens during the exposure.

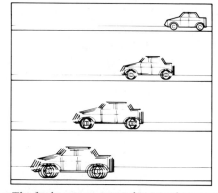

The farther away your subject is, the slower the shutter speed you'll need to blur it. Even at 1/1000 second, a photograph would blur the motion of a car speeding by right in front of the camera; as the distance to the car increased, you'd need slower and slower shutter speeds to get the same effect, and the image would get smaller and smaller.

PANNING
Move with the action

Sometimes the action in a scene is the most important part of it, and you want to emphasize its speed. Sometimes the action is so fast that you can't catch it with even the fastest shutter speeds. This picture was taken with a technique designed for both these situations—panning, moving the camera during the exposure to follow the course of the action. The pictures you take with this technique are expressive and very distinctive: your subject is recorded sharply; everything else is blurred.

Because the effect of panning depends on recording motion, relatively slow shutter speeds are used with this technique. The shutter speed you need to pan a scene, and the amount of blur your picture will record, depend on how fast the action is and how close to it you are. Experiment with various shutter speeds—every picture will be different. To pan a person walking, try 1/30 second; to pan a runner 50 feet away, use 1/60 second; for a runner 20 feet away, use 1/125 second. In this picture, the runners were very large in the frame, and they were moving fast; the photographer

used a speed of 1/500 second to catch them.

The amount of blur in your pictures will also vary if there are different rates of motion in the scene. Here, the first runner is in sharper focus than the others, because he's the one the photographer followed with the camera. The runners' arms and legs are more blurred than their bodies, because they were moving faster than the overall rate of movement, and not in the direction the camera was turning.

Panning is easy to do, but it takes some practice to get good results. Before you take the picture, prepare yourself so you can swing with your camera as the action passes you. Point your feet in the direction you want to finish in, and pivot your body to face the direction where the action will start. When your subject comes into the frame of the viewfinder, swing your whole body to follow the movement, untwisting as you press the shutter release.

Panning can effectively blur background details to isolate your subject. If the photographer hadn't moved the camera here, the feeling of participation would be gone; only the stands behind the runners would be sharp.

● Set your camera in the shutter-preferred mode for panning, or use the manual mode to set both shutter speed and aperture. If your camera is aperture-preferred, you can choose the right shutter speed by adjusting the f-stop until the camera gives you the right speed. Don't use the program mode for panning; it will choose a shutter speed for you.

● Once you've chosen the shutter speed for a pan, adjust your f-stop setting for a correct exposure. Keep the aperture as small as possible for maximum depth of field. You won't have time to focus on your subject, so use the technique of zone focus to get a sharp picture. Focus your camera at the point where you expect your subject to pass in front of you, and concentrate on following the action. Practice by following an imaginary subject with your camera, so you can take the shot without having to think about every step.

● A normal (50mm) or moderate wide-angle lens is best for panning, because it gives you enough background to emphasize the effect of motion. A telephoto lens is much harder to use, because your subject is magnified in the frame and moves across it much more quickly. This picture was taken with a telephoto lens, and required both careful tracking and a high shutter speed—1/500 second.

● A tripod is very useful for panned shots. Set your camera on the tripod and loosen the controls so that the camera swings freely in the direction of the pan, without moving at all in the other direction. Then push the camera to follow the action as you take the picture. Make sure the tripod head is exactly level and the post exactly vertical, or your picture will record the action at an angle.

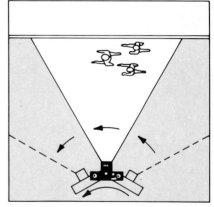

For the best results, pay attention to your follow-through when you pan, to keep your camera trained on the action. The dotted lines show the complete angle of view the photographer covered for this shot.

TIME EXPOSURES
Prolong the impression

Many pictures can be taken only with very long exposures—night scenes, fireworks, building interiors. Wherever there's too little light to record an image on film at a normal shutter speed setting, you can use your camera to make time exposures—to open the shutter for a very long time, so that your photographs record both light and motion.

Most cameras have some shutter speeds for long exposures, such as 1 second or 2 seconds—some automatic cameras have settings of many minutes. All cameras have a B setting—the B stands for bulb— that opens the shutter when you press the shutter release, and holds it open as long as you keep the shutter release depressed. Some cameras also have a T setting, for time, which opens the shutter when you press the shutter release and holds it open until you press the release again. The B setting is convenient for exposures of 10 seconds or less; the T setting is better for longer exposures.

At the very low light levels that make time exposures necessary, your camera's meter is usually not accurate. You'll have to use longer exposures than the meter indicates to get good pictures, and you'll have to experiment with exposure times. If your meter indicates an exposure of 1 to 10 seconds, double that time for a well-exposed picture; from 10 to 100 seconds, triple the time indicated by the meter. With exposures of more than 100 seconds—almost two minutes—your results will be unpredictable; use a very long exposure time to make sure the image is recorded. Use a stop watch or a watch with a second hand to monitor exposure time.

Because you can't rely on your camera meter for an accurate reading when the light is low, set your camera in the manual mode for time exposures. Use fast film, ISO/ASA 200 or above. If you want to record wavy trails of light in a night scene, you can hand-hold the camera for an exposure of up to about 1 second, but for a sharp image, like this well-composed shot of a city street, use a tripod to hold the camera steady.

To photograph fireworks, aim the camera lens at the point where you expect the bursts to appear (X), and leave the shutter open during several explosions. If there are no fixed objects in the picture, move the camera slightly between bursts—first left (A), then right (B)—to fill the frame with color.

● Time exposures can give you effective photographs in many low-light situations. Use them to photograph night traffic, as in this picture, or to record the glow of neon signs. You can also use them when your subject is a source of light in complete darkness—keep the shutter open long enough to record several bursts of a fireworks display, or several bolts of lightning. And anywhere detail and depth of field are important, you can use time exposures to permit the use of a very small aperture.

● The aperture needed for a time exposure depends on your subject. Where you want to record some detail, use a moderate or small aperture; this picture was taken at f/5.6 or f/8, with a shutter speed of 5 to 10 seconds. When your subject is a distant light source, like fireworks, you can use any large aperture; it won't have any effect on the picture. And where detail is important, as it is in the interior of a building, use an aperture of f/16 or f/22.

● When you photograph fireworks, leave the shutter open long enough to record several bursts of color; as long as the sky is dark, it doesn't matter how long your exposure is. Use a normal (50mm) lens or a moderate telephoto or wide-angle lens; a very long lens would limit your picture area too much, and a very short one would make the bursts of light too small.

● Use a tripod to hold the camera steady during a time exposure. For very long exposures where wind is a problem, hang a bag full of heavy stones or water from the center post of the tripod; the weight will help steady it. Always use a cable release to minimize vibration when you press the shutter. Carry a pocket flashlight so you can see to make camera settings and find accessories.

Time exposures are ideal for photographing dimly lighted interiors, where you need to record fine detail. Use an aperture of f/16 or f/22 for maximum depth of field.

THE SELF-TIMER
Get into the picture

This picture was taken with the aid of the self-timer, the camera control that lets you delay the action of the camera's shutter release. With the self-timer, you can set your camera to take a picture and then get into the scene yourself, before it snaps the shot. There's a delay of several seconds—usually from 1 to 9—from the time you activate the control to the time the camera makes the exposure. The self-timer is usually located on the front of the camera; check your manual to see how this control works on your camera.

This picture illustrates the most common use for the self-timer—letting the photographer get into the picture. The self-timer is also useful when the light is low and you don't have a cable release, because it eliminates the vibration your hands can produce when you press the shutter release. In both situations, a tripod or other solid camera support is essential when you use this control—you must be able to set your camera in place to compose the picture, and you must also be able to move away from the camera.

Using the self-timer is simple; your most important consideration is setting up the picture. Whether you're photographing a group of people or you're the only one in the picture, make sure your subject is the most important part of the scene. Frame the shot to eliminate distracting or confusing background details, and try to position people so that they're standing or sitting at different levels, with no one blocking anyone else from the camera. In natural surroundings like these, composition is fairly simple; you can use natural elements to position your subjects creatively. Here, the tree branches keep the interest of the picture centered on the people.

The best pictures are spontaneous, so keep your subjects relaxed. Take a few minutes to talk and get people acting and interacting naturally. When everyone is relaxed, set your camera for the picture—and then react with the rest of the group. Take several shots while you have everyone together, to make sure you get at least one picture everyone will like.

When you include yourself in the picture, be sure to decide on your position before you activate the self-timer. Compose the shot so that you're part of the picture, and use your depth-of-field preview to make sure everyone in the group will be in focus.

● Set your exposure for a self-timed picture as you would for any other shot. When you're photographing a group, use a shutter speed of 1/60 or 1/125 second to freeze any unexpected movements, and an aperture small enough to keep everyone in focus—here, at least f/11. If your camera focuses automatically, it could focus on the background between two people instead of on the people themselves; to prevent this, focus on one person and then lock the focus before you get into the picture.

● The self-timer can also be used indoors for pictures with electronic flash. Set your camera on a tripod, and make sure the shutter speed dial is correctly set for flash. You can use furniture to compose the picture the same way you'd use natural elements, by having some people sitting and others standing—put the children on the floor, where they can take a comfortable and natural pose.

● A normal (50mm) lens is good for group pictures, because it gives you good depth of field and a fairly wide angle of view. Use a moderate wide-angle lens for larger groups, where it's difficult to get everyone into the picture.

● A steady camera support is essential when you use the self-timer in place of a cable release. Once you've composed the picture and set your exposure, set the self-timer and take your hand away from the camera—if you touch the camera during the exposure, the self-timer will not be able to eliminate vibration.

● If you don't have a tripod, you can often improvise a camera support so that you can use the self-timer. A wall, a fence post, or any other solid support can give you a place to work from; for this picture, a tree stump or a rock might have been used.

POLARIZING AND CORRECTION FILTERS
Discover their effects

Filters, thin sheets made of glass, plastic, or gelatin, are used to do three very important things in photography. With the right filter over your camera lens, you can intensify colors in the picture; you can correct color in difficult shooting situations; and you can change the color balance of your film so that you can use it in a different kind of light than it's intended for.

This picture was taken with a polarizing filter, one of the most useful filters you can own. Polarizers make a blue sky darker, and bright colors richer. They can also reduce or eliminate glare on glass, water, polished stone, and other reflective surfaces, and give your pictures more detail in these areas.

Color correction filters are also important. The most commonly used such filter is the 1A or skylight filter, a faint pink lens that can be left on the camera all the time to protect the camera lens. The skylight removes the blue tinge reflected from the blue sky, and warms skin tones and water tones. The 81A (yellow) and the CC10R (light red) filters are used for the same reasons. These filters are stronger than the skylight, and give you a more effective correction.

Color conversion filters are used to balance color slide film to a noncompatible light source. When you use daylight film in artificial light, use a blue 80A filter to prevent an orange or yellow cast in your pictures. When you shoot with tungsten film in natural light, you can prevent extreme blueness in your pictures by using an amber 85B filter. No film is balanced for fluorescent light, so you'll need an FLD filter to eliminate a green cast and keep the colors natural when you use daylight film in this light.

All filters absorb some of the light that enters the camera lens, so a filtered photograph requires more exposure—a slower shutter speed, a larger aperture, or both—than an unfiltered one. Your camera will probably automatically compensate for this difference in exposure; check your camera manual, and follow the instructions that come with the filter.

- If your camera meter reads through the lens, it will automatically give you the correct exposure with a filter; you don't have to use the exposure factors marked on the filter. To make sure you get the correct exposure, set your camera according to your manual; any exceptions will be noted.

- Filters are sold in sizes to fit specific lenses, and in Series sizes that use an adapter ring to attach a universal filter holder to any camera lens. If you want to buy individual filters, buy them to fit your most used camera lens; you may be able to use adapter rings to make them usable with your other lenses.

- A polarizing filter is most useful when the light is from a single source, coming from an angle of 90 degrees to the camera. This filter is built into a rotating mount. Rotate the filter as you look through the camera lens to find the position where it will be most effective, and take your exposure reading with the filter in this position. The polarizing filter is not effective on overcast days.

- Use a skylight (1A) filter or an 81A filter to eliminate blueness from snow scenes and on heavily overcast days. At high altitudes, use an 81A filter to cut the haze. If you photograph at high altitudes regularly, invest in a UV haze filter for maximum correction.

- When you're photographing in a situation where there are several different light sources, use a film balanced for the dominant source—daylight film for natural light or electronic flash, tungsten film for incandescent light. In fluorescent light, use daylight film with an FLD filter, or tungsten film with an FLB. If you're using electronic flash in fluorescent light, usually no filter is needed.

In open shade (shaded area), light reflected from the sky can give a blue tinge to your pictures, and make skin tones look unnatural. Use a skylight (1A) filter to correct the color; if there's a pronounced green tinge from foliage, use a CC10R for maximum correction. Keep a lens hood on the camera lens to prevent flare.

SPECIAL-EFFECTS FILTERS
Experiment for many moods

Special-effects filters, used over your camera lens, can create striking and imaginative photographs. You can use these filters to make sunsets surrealistic, shatter points of light into brilliant stars, and make everyday portraits misty and romantic. Used alone or combined, special-effects filters are an exciting tool for experimentation.

Some of the most common of these filters are color filters, star and diffraction filters, and diffusion filters, usually called fog filters. This picture was taken with a strong magenta filter and a diffraction star filter; it combines two effects.

Strongly colored filters are normally used for black-and-white photography. When you photograph in color, you can use them to change the overall color of the scene, as in this picture. There are also varicolored filters, shaded from one color to another or from a color to clear—from side to side of the filter or from the center to the edges. You can rotate these filters on the camera lens to get the effect you want in your picture.

Star filters can add excitement to many ordinary shots; they create a starburst around any hard light in the picture. This effect is caused by a pattern of crisscross lines etched on the filter; a star is formed at every point where the lines intersect. The number of points on each star depends on the pattern of lines. Diffraction or rainbow filters create a similar effect; they spread any hard light into a rainbow-like spectrum.

Diffusion filters can give you a wide variety of special effects. Very light fog filters just soften the image slightly; they're popular for portraits, because they soften facial features and add romantic overtones. More extreme fog filters can create a heavy fog throughout the scene, and some filters are graded so that only the center of the picture is sharp. Fog filters work best in low light, when you're using a large aperture. In this situation, light colors will seem to glow.

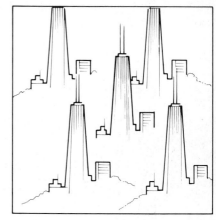

Split-image filters, among the most complex of special-effects filters, split the picture into separate or overlapping images, in bands or concentric circles, to give you a multiple image. Since this filter repeats everything in the picture, it's best used when the background is very simple.

● Like polarizing and correction filters, special-effects filters absorb some of the light entering the camera lens, and you'll have to compensate for this in your exposures. Your camera will probably do this automatically; check your manual for specifics. Follow the instructions that come with the filters to make sure you get the correct exposure.

● Many different types of special-effects filters are available; ask your photo dealer for more information. Like color correction filters, special-effects filters are sold to fit individual lenses and in Series sizes that use adapter rings to fit any lens. Some filter manufacturers offer interchangeable filter holders and kits that let you make your own color combinations.

● You can improvise some special-effects filters with materials you have on hand. Inexpensive sheets of colored acetate can be used in place of color filters; hold the acetate directly over the camera lens. Use a piece of window screen or nylon mesh to get four-pointed stars, or lay two pieces of screen together at an angle of 45 degrees to each other to get eight-pointed stars. You can make your own diffusion filter by gently smearing petroleum jelly over a clear piece of glass and holding it in front of the camera lens, jelly side away from the lens.

● When you use two or more filters together, the corners of your picture may be darkened or cut off, as they are here. This effect, called vignetting, is especially noticeable with wide-angle lenses. If you plan your shots to take advantage of it, vignetting can add to the effect of your pictures.

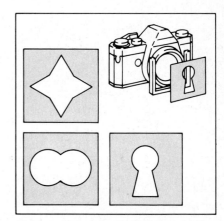

You can get another kind of special effect with a shape frame, a plastic frame that fits over the camera lens and uses stencil-like cutouts to frame your pictures in special shapes. A wide variety of shapes is available—keyholes, stars, ovals, circles, hearts, and combinations. Experiment with various shapes to get different effects.

ON-CAMERA FLASH
Add light to the picture

Whether you're photographing in darkness or daylight, indoors or out, an electronic flash is one of the most useful camera accessories you can own. With a flash, you can add just enough light to the scene to get a perfect picture.

The electronic flash is a separate unit that connects to your camera at the hot shoe, located at the top of most cameras. The hot shoe connects the flash to your camera's shutter mechanism, synchronizing the two so that the flash goes off when you press the shutter release. Automatic flash units read the light in the scene just as the camera meter does, and require similar adjustments to give you a correct exposure.

There are three types of electronic flash units, and each type is adjusted differently. Manual flash units require that you calculate the proper f-stop setting for the flash, based on the distance to your subject. Automatic flash units read the light in the scene and adjust the length of the flash for a correct exposure; you set the f-stop and the ISO/ASA of your film on both the camera and the flash. Dedicated flash units are the easiest to use; they give you the correct flash automatically.

The electronic flash can be used to add light to an overall scene where there isn't enough light to permit a fast shutter speed or a small aperture, and you don't want to make a time exposure. It can also be used to reduce contrast, even in bright light; this is called fill flash. In the picture of the swimmers here, the faces would have been in shadow without the flash, because of the strong backlighting on the water.

The electronic flash produces very strong, harsh light, with no shadows on your subject and dark shadows in the background. Flash pictures have little depth, because only objects at the same distance from the flash will be evenly lighted—objects closer to the camera will be brighter, and objects farther away will be dark, like the background in this picture of the Indian dancer.

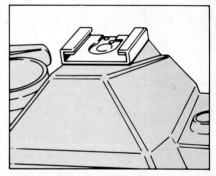

The hot shoe, located at the top of the camera, connects the flash unit to the shutter mechanism. The flash unit simply slides into the hot shoe.

You can illuminate a wider area and create softer shadows by bouncing the flash off a light-colored ceiling or wall, so that it's reflected back onto your subjects at an angle. A white ceiling absorbs light, so with an eight-foot ceiling, allow at least two f-stops more exposure than your flash calculations indicate.

● Every camera has a shutter speed setting synchronized for use with electronic flash—usually 1/60 or 1/125 second. This speed may be marked in a different color or may be indicated by an X or a lightning-bolt symbol.

● The correct exposure for a flash picture depends on the power of the unit and the distance from the camera to your subject. Nondedicated flash units give you a set of guide numbers or a calculator dial to help you choose the correct f-stop. To use the calculator dial, set the film speed; the dial will show possible combinations of f-stops and subject distances. To use the guide number, choose the number for the film you're using and divide by the distance to your subject in feet; this gives you the f-number required. Check your flash manual for specific instructions.

● The light from an electronic flash is very harsh, and can produce disturbing shadows. Keep your subjects at the same distance from the camera, and keep bright objects out of the near foreground. To see how the light will fall when you take the picture, you can trigger your flash unit without releasing the shutter.

● Electronic flash can be used to stop action when your subject is within 10 to 15 feet of the camera, because the flash duration is very short—as little as 1/10,000 second. It's also useful for multiple exposures, discussed earlier in this book. For a different effect, you can use a slow shutter speed instead of the camera's sync speed; your picture will record one sharp image and a blur.

● Direct flash will cause glare on reflective surfaces in the scene—mirrors, framed pictures, even a person's glasses. To prevent these hot spots of bright light, compose your pictures carefully, and point the camera at an angle to reflective surfaces. Have people look a little to one side to decrease the likelihood of pink eyes in the picture.

OFF-CAMERA FLASH
Extend the light, soften the shadows

Electronic flash is usually used on the camera, but in many situations, you can get better pictures by taking your flash unit off the camera. On-camera flash is harsh, and usually gives you pictures with very hard light and very dark shadows. Direct flash also limits your pictures to one main subject, because only objects at the same distance from the camera will be evenly lighted. With off-camera flash, you can solve both of these problems, for more natural light and more even light throughout your pictures.

When you use your flash unit separately from your camera, it doesn't attach to the camera's hot shoe. Instead, it's connected to a terminal called the PC terminal, by means of a flash synchronization or PC cord. The PC cord links the flash to the camera shutter the same way the hot shoe does. Dedicated flash units are an exception; because they're linked directly to the camera's exposure controls through the hot shoe, they must be connected with an adapter to the hot shoe—not the PC terminal—for off-camera use.

Careful positioning of the flash unit is essential for good results with off-camera flash. Where you have several subjects, the flash should be equidistant from them. Off-camera flash gives you a very good range of light, so you can include people at varying distances from the camera—look at the three graduates in this picture. But the flash unit must be roughly the same distance from each person, or the light in the picture will be uneven.

The height and angle of the flash are also important. Raise the flash unit to eye level or above; if the light is low, the effect will be unnatural and spooky, and the background may show large shadows. A head-on flash will give you a flat, harsh light with no shadows; you can give the picture a more natural look by moving the unit to an angle of 10 degrees or more to the side. Experiment with the flash at various positions to get the effect you want—a shallow angle produces slight shadows; a greater angle produces larger shadows over a wider area.

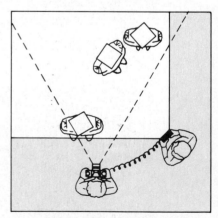

The PC terminal on the camera is used to make the connection between the camera and the flash unit; a PC cord links the two pieces of equipment.

● The correct exposure for a picture with off-camera flash is calculated the same way as for on-camera flash, but the distance used for the calculation is the distance between the flash unit and the subject, rather than between the camera and the subject. Set your camera for flash-synchronized shutter speed. If you have a dedicated flash, this is the only preparation required; if you have a nondedicated unit, you must also set the f-stop and the ISO/ASA of your film on both the camera and the flash. Use the calculator dial or the guide numbers on your flash unit to determine the correct f-stop for the picture; check your flash manual for specific instructions.

● To soften the shadows in a flash-lighted scene, use a sheet of white cardboard to diffuse some of the light and redirect it where it will be most useful. Hold the reflector off to the side of the flash, so that it catches the light and bounces it back onto your subject's face. Keep your subject far enough from the background to prevent shadows from falling on it; if the background is close, use a reflector card and hold the flash as high as you can to soften the light.

● The standard PC cord is usually about 8 to 10 inches long, but cords up to 25 feet long are available at many camera stores. A long PC cord is very useful, because it gives you freedom of movement and flexibility in positioning the flash. Cords sometimes fail, so it's a good idea to carry a spare.

● To hold your flash unit off-camera, you can simply raise it as high as possible, or have a friend hold it in the right position while you take the picture. You can also use a mounting bracket or flange, available from your camera dealer, to clamp the unit into place for your shot.

For even illumination over the depth of the picture, position the flash so that it's equidistant from all your subjects. For this photograph, an assistant held the flash. If you set the flash within the picture area, be sure it isn't visible in the picture.

CAMERA HANDLING
Basic photography techniques

Every camera is different, so read your camera manual carefully and follow its instructions exactly. These procedures are typical for most 35mm cameras.

Loading Film
Open the back of the camera, usually by lifting the film rewind knob and pulling out the back, or by releasing a catch on the side of the camera. With the rewind knob up, fit the film canister—recessed end up—into the chamber on the left side under the rewind knob, with the tail of the film on top and extending to the right. Push the stem of the rewind knob back down to lock the canister into place.

Pull the tail of the film gently out of the canister and insert it into the slot in the take-up spool, at the right side of the camera. Turn the rewind knob slightly to make sure the film is snug against the sprockets, and advance the film once to make sure that it's straight and that the sprockets are engaged. Close the camera and advance the film twice more.

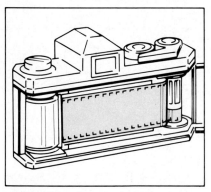
Loading film.

The Film Counter
The film counter for most cameras is on the right side of the camera, next to the film advance lever. Many counters have a

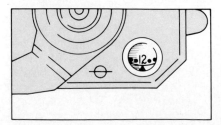
The film counter.

red zone at the beginning of the roll of film, which indicates that you still have some exposed film left in the chamber. Advance your film until the number 1 comes up on the counter; the camera back must be closed.

The Advance/Rewind Controls
The film advance lever must be fully cocked before the shutter can be released. The rewind knob should turn slightly every time you advance the film; check it periodically throughout the roll to make sure it's still turning. Never jerk the advance lever, especially in very cold weather; this could break the film or cause static marks on it.

The film advance lever.

Unloading Film
Release the take-up spool by pushing the film rewind button on the bottom of the camera, under the advance lever. Pull the rewind lever out and turn it slowly clockwise until you feel the film pull loose from the take-up spool. Turn the lever a few more times and then open the camera back to remove the film canister. Always load and unload film in a shady place, or with your back to the sun.

The Viewfinder Display
Manual cameras indicate whether you need more or less light for an exposure; shutter-preferred cameras indicate the required aperture; aperture-preferred cameras indicate the required shutter speed. Some cameras show both f-stop and shutter speed settings, as well as other information. Check your camera manual to see what information your viewfinder provides.

Some cameras use LCD displays. These displays are very sensitive to heat, and will black out at high temperatures. Try to keep light out of the viewfinder while you're

making an exposure; this will change your meter reading.

Focusing
Most 35mm cameras with through-the-lens focusing have a matte glass screen with a central microprism ring and a split-image spot in the middle. To bring an object into focus, adjust the focusing ring on the lens until all three parts of the screen show a sharp image. When the image is in focus, the microprism pattern will disappear and straight lines that pass through the split-image spot will be unbroken.

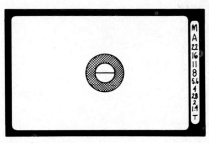
The focusing screen.

The Battery Check
Most cameras have a battery check to indicate whether the batteries are good. Always check the batteries before you use your camera, and always carry a spare battery. Meter displays and depth-of-field previews drain your battery, so don't leave them on when you aren't using them. Bright sunlight and cold weather also cause the batteries to drain faster.

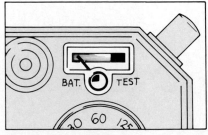
The battery check.

Holding the Camera
To minimize the effects of camera shake, hold your camera on your left palm, with your thumb and first two fingers around the lens barrel within easy reach of the focusing and f-stop rings. Use your right

hand to hold the camera steady, with your right index finger on the shutter release. Keep your elbows down at your sides or in against your chest. Spread your feet apart slightly and keep your knees bent and flexible. Let your breath out just before you take the picture, and press the shutter release gently.

Holding the camera horizontally.

To hold the camera vertically, rest it on your cupped left hand, and steady it with your right hand from above. Use your left thumb and fingers to turn the focusing dial, and your right index finger to press the shutter release. Leave your camera strap around your neck and wrap the slack around your wrist to help steady the camera.

Holding the camera vertically.

Protecting Your Camera

To protect your camera from heat, keep it out of direct sunlight, and don't leave it in a closed car or glove compartment. In hot climates, keep film in an insulated chest or wrapped in a white reflective cloth. Have exposed film processed immediately, or store it in the refrigerator, wrapped in plastic.

To protect your camera from cold weather, keep it under your jacket when you aren't shooting; extreme cold can cause the film to become brittle enough to tear or break. Advance and rewind the film very gently in extreme cold to prevent static marks and breakage.

Water, especially salt water, will damage your equipment, so make sure your camera is fully protected. Keep either a skylight (1A) or a polarizing filter over the lens. Slip the camera into a plastic bag with the lens barrel poked through one side, and secure the plastic around the lens with a rubber band. Reach up inside the bag to operate the controls. If you take the camera on a boat, tie it to your neck or wrist; the neck strap can slip over your head if you fall. Watertight camera bags are available.

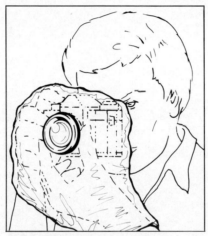

Protecting your camera.

Cleaning Your Camera

The only parts of the camera that need regular cleaning are the lens, filters, and film chamber. To clean the film chamber, blow out the dust periodically with a syringe or a can of compressed air. You can also use a soft camel-hair brush for dusting. Keep the outside of the camera, especially the moving parts, free of dust.

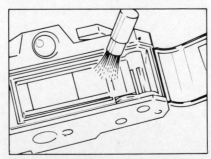

Cleaning your camera.

Clean lenses and filters with special lens cleaning fluid and lens tissues, available in camera stores. Don't use water or tissues made for any other purpose; they will scratch the lens.

The Basic Camera Outfit

As you take more pictures in more varied circumstances, you may want to invest in additional camera equipment. There are dozens of lenses, filters, and other accessories for most 35mm SLR cameras, but you'll be fully equipped and prepared for any picture with this basic outfit. Start with a lens hood and a tripod; add filters and lenses as you can afford them.

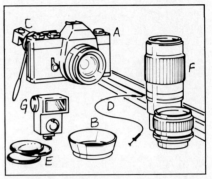

The basic camera outfit.

- Camera body with normal (50mm) lens. (A)
- Rubber lens hood, to protect the lens from shock and glare. (B)
- Tripod, to steady the camera with slow shutter speeds. A lightweight tripod with telescoping legs is good for traveling. (C)
- Cable release, to prevent camera shake when you press the shutter release at slow shutter speeds. (D)
- Filters: skylight (1A) for eliminating blue in shade or snow; polarizing filter for intensifying colors and reducing glare; FLD for correcting color in fluorescent light. (E)
- Lenses: close-up lenses (+1, +2, +3); moderate telephoto or telephoto zoom (135mm to 200mm); moderate wide-angle (28mm). If you don't want to buy a wide-angle lens, you can use a wide-angle adapter that screws on the front of your normal lens. (F)
- Electronic flash unit (optional). (G)
- Camera bag, to hold all equipment, cleaning supplies, extra film, plastic bags and twist fasteners, paper and pencil, pocket flashlight, and a small screwdriver.

Glossary

Angle of view. The angle formed between the lens and the most widely separated points in a scene that the lens takes in.

Aperture. The lens opening through which light can pass.
See also **f-stop.**

ASA. *See* **Film speed.**

Automatic camera. A camera in which all or part of the task of exposure determination and control is performed by built-in components. Some cameras are completely automatic and give the photographer no control over exposure. More versatile cameras can be controlled manually or set to one or more modes of automatic operation. These modes include:
Aperture-preferred (aperture-priority). The photographer chooses an aperture (f-stop) setting for the lens; the camera chooses an appropriate shutter speed, based on the film speed it's set for and the reading of the light meter in the camera.
Shutter-preferred (shutter-priority). The photographer chooses a shutter speed setting; the camera chooses an appropriate lens aperture setting.
Program. The camera chooses both a shutter speed and a lens aperture; the photographer has no exposure control.
See also **Manual camera.**

Automatic flash. An electronic flash unit with a photoelectric eye, which monitors light reflected from the subject and shuts off the flash when enough light has been received for proper exposure, according to the speed of the film and the f-stop setting of the lens. Autoflash allows the photographer to use a single f-stop setting over a range of distances between flash and subject; manually controlled flash units require that the f-stop be adjusted for every change in distance.
See also **Guide number.**

Bracketing. Making exposures at greater and lesser exposure settings than those indicated by a meter reading of the subject, by varying the lens aperture or the shutter speed or both. Bracketing is used to ensure at least one properly exposed shot when conditions make it hard to be sure the meter reading is accurate.

Bounce light, bounce flash. Light, usually electronic flash, aimed at a surface such as a white wall, ceiling, or reflector card so that it's reflected back onto the subject.

Cable release, cable shutter release. A flexible cable with a plunger needle running through the center. The cable release screws into the shutter release of a camera, and is used to trip the shutter without having to touch the camera directly. This prevents any possibility of camera movement from finger pressure.

Close-up lens. *See* **Supplementary lens.**

Color balance. The relative sensitivity of the layers of color film emulsion to various colors of light. White light is composed of light of different colors and wavelengths; to record natural-looking colors, the film color balance must match that of the light falling on the subject. Color balance is usually expressed as an equivalent color temperature, measured in units called Kelvins (K). There are three types of color film balance:
Daylight. Balanced to match daylight and electronic flash (5500 K).
Tungsten Type B. Balanced to match light with a color temperature of 3200 K. Most indoor color films are tungsten Type B.
Tungsten Type A. Balanced to match light with a color temperature of 3400 K. There is only one film of this type, Kodachrome 40 film 5070.
Either type of tungsten film, Type A or Type B, can be used to take pictures in artificial light.

Color correction filter. A filter that corrects the color reproduction in a photograph when lighting conditions would cause haze or color distortion. The most commonly used such filter is the skylight (1A) filter. Other filters include the 81A and CC10R, used like the skylight; and the ultraviolet (UV) filter, used to cut haze.

Conversion filter. A filter that corrects the color reproduction of film when it is used with lighting that does not match its color balance. Common conversion filters include:
85B filter. Corrects color when a tungsten Type B color film is used with daylight or electronic flash.
85 filter. Corrects color when a tungsten Type A color film is used with daylight or electronic flash.
80A filter. Corrects color when a daylight color film is used with 3200 K tungsten (Type B) lighting.
80B filter. Corrects color when a daylight color film is used with 3400 K tungsten (Type A) lighting.
FLD filter. Corrects color when daylight film is used with fluorescent lighting.
See also **Color balance, Fluorescent light.**

Critical focus. The technique of focusing on the most important part of the subject when depth of field is very limited, thus retaining visual meaning in the photograph. Critical focus is most often used for close-ups, where depth of field is extremely limited and speed is not required.

Daylight film. A type of color film balanced to produce natural-looking colors when used in daylight or with electronic flash.
See also **Color balance, Conversion filter.**

Dedicated flash. An electronic flash unit that connects directly to the camera meter and controls through the hot shoe. These units produce a flash calculated for a correct exposure, according to the speed of the film and the f-stop setting of the lens. Dedicated flash requires no separate adjustments to the flash. Often the flash ready light is displayed in the viewfinder.

Depth of field. The zone in which details remain sharp both in front of and behind the specific point at which the lens is focused. Some single-lens reflex cameras have a *depth-of-field preview* control that lets the photographer see the depth of field in the viewfinder. Most lenses have a depth-of-field scale adjacent to the distance-focusing scale.
Generally, the higher the number of the f-stop, the smaller the lens aperture and the greater the depth of field. To increase depth of field, use a smaller (higher number) f-stop, change to a shorter focal length lens, or move farther away from the subject. To decrease depth of field, use a larger (lower number) f-stop, change to a longer focal length lens, or move closer to the subject.
See also **f-stop.**

DIN. *See* **Film speed.**

Direct flash. Flash illumination aimed directly at the subject. Direct flash is intense, and produces hard-edged, dark shadows. It provides maximum definition of texture and details.

Electronic flash. A flash unit that generates light in a gas-filled glass tube by the discharge of current between two electrodes. Power may be supplied by batteries or by AC current, depending on the design of the unit; many electronic flash units can use both kinds of power. An electronic flash burst is much shorter than that of a flashbulb—typically, from 1/750 second to 1/10,000 second, depending on the kind of tube and the power supply. Electronic flash lighting is color-balanced for use with daylight-type color films, 5500 K.
See also **Automatic flash, Dedicated flash.**

Exposure. The amount of light that reaches a film; the combined effect of how much light strikes the film, controlled by the aperture or f-stop, and for how long, controlled by the shutter speed. The exposure required in any particular situation varies according to the speed (sensitivity) of the film used.
See also **Film speed.**

Exposure memory lock. A control on automatic cameras that permits holding or locking in the exposure reading or setting taken in one situation while the camera is moved to another situation. The memory lock is most often used to take and hold close-up meter readings while the camera is moved back for a fuller view of the subject.

Exposure meter, light meter. A device that measures the amount of light falling on or reflected off a subject, relates it to film speed, and indicates shutter speed and f-stop settings that will produce a normal degree of exposure on the film. There are two basic types:
Reflected-light meter. Measures the light reflected from the subject. Used to take a reading from the camera angle of view, either at the camera distance or closer to the subject. Built-in meters are reflected-light meters. *Averaging meters* read the light in the entire scene and average it; *center-weighted meters* put greater emphasis on an area covering about 40 percent of the frame, at the center. *Spot meters* read only a small circle at the center of the frame.
Incident-light meter. Measures the light falling on the subject. Used to take a reading at the subject position, with the light-collecting cell of the meter aimed toward the camera position.

Film speed. A rating of the sensitivity of a film to light, used to determine the required exposure. Until recently, film speeds have been rated by a series of ASA numbers (American Standards Association) and a series of DIN numbers (Deutsche Industrie Norm, the European standard)—for example, ASA/DIN 400/27. Camera controls were marked accordingly. Currently, however, film speed ratings are being standardized to a series of ISO numbers (International Standards Organization), corresponding to the previously used ASA numbers.

A doubling of the ISO/ASA number indicates a film that's twice as sensitive to light, the equivalent of one f-stop difference in exposure. DIN numbers are logarithmic; an increase of three indicates a doubling of film speed. *Slow films* range from ISO 25 (ASA/DIN 25/15) to ISO 32 (ASA/DIN 32/16); *medium films* range from ISO 64 (ASA/DIN 64/19) to ISO 160 (ASA/DIN 160/23). *Fast films* are rated ISO 200 (ASA/DIN 200/24) or above.

Filter. A transparent material that absorbs some wavelengths of the light passing through it; used with a lens or a light source to change the color balance of the light. Filters are commonly used to intensify colors and reduce glare and reflections; to correct color reproduction when lighting conditions would cause haze or color distortion; and to correct the color balance between film and lighting. Filters are usually made of glass, plastic, or thin gelatin sheets.
Special-effects filters are filters used to produce an unusual effect. Color filters, normally used in black-and-white photography, are used for special effects in color photography; they may be a single color or of varied colors, of uniform or graduated density. Many special-effect devices called filters are actually optical-distorting devices that do not absorb wavelengths, but change the path of the image-forming rays of light. These devices can be used to produce stars, rainbow dispersions of white light, multiple images, apparent fog, and many other effects.
See also **Color correction filter, Conversion filter, Polarizing filter.**

Flare. Light reflected inside a lens or camera, causing noticeable differences of exposure in certain parts of the picture; also, the effect of this light as visible on the film. Flare is usually caused by a direct light source within or very close to the lens field of view. A lens hood is the best protection against flare.

Fluorescent light. Light produced by any of the various types of fluorescent tubes. Fluorescent light is not color-balanced with any type of color film, and gives an overall blue-green or yellow-green cast to photographs unless a color correction filter is used over the camera lens. The filter required for natural-looking color depends on the type of film:
Daylight film. Use an FLD (or CFD) filter over the lens, and allow one f-stop more exposure than the meter indicates.
Tungsten Type B film. Use an FLB (or CFB) filter, and allow one f-stop more exposure than the meter indicates.
Tungsten Type A film. Use an FLB (or CFB) filter plus an 82A filter, and allow one f-stop more exposure than the meter indicates.
See also **Color balance.**

Focal length. An optical measurement of a basic lens property; the distance between the optical center of the lens and the film when the lens is focused at infinity. Focal length determines the angle of view and the degree of magnification a lens produces; it is usually expressed in millimeters. Lenses are commonly grouped according to a general classification of focal length:
Normal lens. One with a focal length approximately equal to the diagonal measurement across the negative. A 50mm lens is considered a normal lens for a 35mm camera; a 25mm to 40mm lens is normal for a 110 or 126 cartridge camera. A normal lens produces a perspective and degree of magnification similar to that seen by the human eye.
Telephoto lens. One with a longer focal length and a narrower angle of view than a normal lens. It permits focusing at greater distances from the subject, and produces greater magnification. For 35mm cameras, telephoto lenses have focal lengths of 75mm or 80mm and longer.
Wide-angle lens. One with a shorter focal length and, therefore, a wider angle of view than a normal lens. Wide-angle lenses for 35mm cameras have focal lengths of about 35mm and shorter. They permit focusing at shorter distances from the subject than a normal lens, but produce less magnification from a given camera position.
See also **Zoom lens.**

f-stop, f-number. The designation of lens aperture settings; also, the camera control that determines f-stop. The standard series is f/1, f/1.4, f/2, f/2.8, f/4, f/5.6, f/8, f/11, f/16, f/22, f/32. Some lenses do not cover the full range of settings; others may extend to higher numbers. The lower (smaller) the number, the greater the diameter of the aperture, and the more light will strike the film. Changing from one f-stop to the next lower f-number doubles the amount of light passing through the lens; changing to the next higher f-number halves it.

Guide number. A number that relates the light output of a flash unit to a particular film speed. The guide number can be used to determine the required exposure for a flash picture. Divide the guide number for the film you're using by the distance in feet from the flash unit to the subject; the result is the f-stop setting to be used on the lens. The guide number is different for films of different speeds; if you know the number for only one film speed, you can use higher or lower f-stops for faster or slower film.

Hot shoe. The flash contact on a camera with built-in electrical contacts. When a flash unit with a corresponding *hot foot* is plugged into the hot shoe, the unit is automatically connected with the camera's shutter synchronizing system.

ISO. *See* **Film speed.**

Light meter. *See* **Exposure meter.**

Macro lens. A lens that allows focusing at very short distances from the subject; a specially designed close-up lens.

Manual camera. A camera in which the task of exposure determination and control is performed entirely by the photographer. Some automatic cameras have a manual mode or override to permit manual operation.
See also **Automatic camera.**

Mode. An operational setting that determines how much of the task of exposure determination and control is performed by the camera. Many automatic cameras have two or more modes.
See also **Automatic camera, Manual camera.**

Motor drive. A camera accessory that advances the film and, in 35mm cameras, cocks the shutter automatically; also called a power film advance. Most motor drives are battery-powered; a few use spring-driven mechanisms. An *auto-winder* is a type of motor drive that advances the film only one frame at a time.

Normal lens. Most commonly, a 50mm lens.
See also **Focal length.**

Panning. Photographing rapid action by swinging the camera left or right to follow a moving subject. A picture taken with this technique shows a blurred background and a sharp image of the subject.

PC terminal. The cord contact on a camera with built-in electrical connections, used to connect a flash unit by means of a *PC cord.* When the flash unit is plugged into the PC terminal with a PC cord, the unit is automatically connected with the camera's shutter mechanism.

Polarizing filter. A filter that absorbs light traveling in one plane and transmits light traveling in other planes. Used to intensify colors and reduce glare and reflected images on reflective surfaces, without changing the color composition of the picture. The polarizing filter also deepens the color of the sky by removing scattered glare.

Selective focus. The technique of focusing on one particular part of a photograph and using a large lens aperture to limit the depth of field in the picture to that area. Selective focus is used to emphasize the most important subject by blurring other objects partially or completely.

Self-timer. A camera control that delays the firing of the shutter after the release is depressed, typically from 1 to 9 seconds. It permits the photographer to make last-minute adjustments or move into the picture after releasing the shutter, and can also be used to reduce camera vibration for long exposures.

Shutter. The device in a camera that controls the length of the exposure. There are two basic types of shutters: the *between-lens shutter,* located inside or just behind the lens; and the *focal-plane shutter,* located in the camera just in front of the film. The focal-plane shutter is generally faster; this is the type used in 35mm SLR cameras.

Shutter-preferred, shutter-priority. *See* **Automatic camera.**

Shutter release. The camera control that causes the shutter to operate. On most cameras the shutter release is a button, which is depressed by finger pressure or by means of a screw-in cable device.
See also **Cable release.**

Shutter speed. The length of time during which light will pass through a lens when the shutter is released; also, the camera control that determines shutter speed. The standard shutter speeds are 1 second and the following fractions of a second: 1/2, 1/4, 1/8, 1/15, 1/30, 1/60, 1/125, 1/250, 1/500, and 1/1000. These speeds are indicated on the control as 1, 2, 4, 8, 15, 30, 60, 125, 250, 500, and 1000. Some shutters may have slower and faster settings.
See also **Time exposure.**

Skylight filter. A filter that absorbs ultraviolet light; used to reduce haze and excessively blue color reproduction. The commonly used skylight filter is a 1A filter; the 81A and CC10R filters produce a stronger correction.
See also **Filter.**

SLR. Single-lens reflex. A type of camera in which a mirror, set at an angle behind the lens, reflects the image up to a viewfinder; the mirror swings out of the way when the shutter is released. SLR cameras have two major advantages: they show exactly what the lens sees, avoiding the difference in viewpoint called parallax; and they permit unlimited interchangeability of lenses.

Strobe. A slang term for electronic flash.

Supplementary lens, auxiliary lens. A simple lens placed in front of a camera lens to change its focal length. Close-up lenses and portrait attachments are supplementary lenses. A positive (+) supplementary lens permits focusing at a shorter than normal distance; the strength of a supplementary lens increases with its power: +1, +2, and so on.

Sync, synchronization. The timing relationship between the camera shutter and a flash unit. Electronic flash requires X synchronization; otherwise the unit will fire too soon or too late. Some cameras also provide M or FP sync for use with various flashbulbs. For proper operation, 35mm SLRs—and any other cameras with a focal-plane shutter—must also be set for the correct sync speed. This is usually 1/60 second, although some cameras provide electronic flash sync at 1/90 or 1/125 second.

Time exposure. An exposure made over a longer period of time than standard shutter speeds permit; used in dim light, at night, or, with a small lens aperture, to record motion. Most cameras have one or two settings for time exposures:
B setting. The most common time exposure control. The shutter opens when the shutter release is pressed and stays open as long as the pressure is maintained. The B stands for bulb, from the time when flash bulbs were not synchronized with the shutter.
T setting. The shutter opens when the shutter release is pressed and stays open until the release is pressed a second time. The T setting is used for very long exposures; T stands for time.

Telephoto lens. *See* **Focal length.**

Tungsten film. A type of color film balanced to produce natural-looking colors when used with tungsten light.
See also **Color balance.**

Tungsten light. Light produced by bulbs that contain a tungsten filament. Household light bulbs are tungsten lamps with a color temperature from about 2200 K to 3000 K, depending on their wattage. Photographic tungsten lamps have a color temperature of 3200 K or 3400 K.
See also **Color balance, Conversion filter.**

Wide-angle lens. *See* **Focal length.**

Zone focusing. The technique of presetting focus to a given point and choosing an f-stop that will provide a useful amount of depth of field in front of and behind that point, thus providing a range or zone of sharp focus rather than a single point. Zone focusing is used for action photographs, when the subject of the picture is moving.
See also **Depth of field.**

Zoom lens. A lens that can be adjusted to any of a range of continuously variable focal lengths. A true zoom lens maintains sharp focus as you change focal length; a vari-focus lens is similar, but requires refocusing with each change of focal length. The zoom ratio of a lens is the ratio between its shortest and longest focal length settings. Zoom lenses are available in a wide variety of focal lengths, from extreme wide-angle to extreme telephoto. Common zoom focal length ranges are 35mm to 85mm, 70mm to 200mm, and 200mm to 600mm.

Photo credits